ACKNOWLEDGEMENTS

When managing editor Pam Art called me to see if I was interested in updating some of Jay Shelton's work to include new woodburning technology, I was eager to accept the challenge. When it was decided that it was really time for a new woodburning book to speak to "the next generation of woodburners," I took a deep breath and then took the plunge. We had just moved into and were still working on our new house and Mason, our second child, was born.

The writing and research were another ball in the air and the juggling act was only possible with the help and support of my wife Phoebe, who managed to watch two little ones, answer my business phone, and put up with the disorganization of an unfinished house while I spent "spare" time on this project.

I am grateful to the folks at Storey who, knowing that this was my first book, were willing to clean up the text so that I could concentrate on content, and especially Mary Twitchell whose own experience as a woodheat author enabled her to look at things from the inside as well as out. I learned what "heavy editing" meant as my sometimes random writing took a much more readable shape.

I would like to thank the people in research who have taken the time and effort to apply modern technology to the ancient science of fire and help keep woodburning an appropriate technology in today's world, especially "Skip" Hayden of Canada and Stockton "Skip" Barnett of Omni Labs in Oregon. Much of the research that accounts for clean combustion principles and sound woodburning practices adopted today was done by Dr. Jay Shelton. His books *Wood Heat Safety* and *Solid Fuels Encyclopedia* are invaluable reference works on the subject.

The OPEC oil embargo of the 70s was an annoying and difficult time, especially for those in northern climes who saw their annual heating bill go from a few hundred to over a thousand dollars. Although the belief that an imminent oil shortage turned out to be a myth, we were reminded that this fossil fuel that we are so dependent upon is after all, a finite energy source. Unfortunately, it takes such occurrences to wake up nations as well as individuals and hopefully precipitate the inevitable changes that are always with us. It is my hope that energy and environmental issues will precede political manipulation and become universally rallied around. Then perhaps the necessary changes will be pro-active instead of re-active.

TABLE OF CONTENTS

Introduction

The other day I caught my four-year-old daughter, Hannah, gazing out the window. "What are you looking at?" I asked her. "The trees," she replied from some faraway place.

I had probably caught her daydreaming, but I took her at her word and looked out myself at the hedgerow of mature maple, cherry, beech, and yellow birch that borders the south side of our field. I decided that this might be a good opportunity to have a short lesson on our newly leafed friends.

"You know, trees are very special," I began.

"Uh, huh." She was still staring out the window.

"They help us in so many ways," I continued.

"Uh, huh."

Then I began to list their earthly virtues. "They shade us from the hot summer sun."

"Uh, huh."

"They are homes for many birds and little animals."

"Uh, huh." She sat still, transfixed by some scene that was being played out in the view through her bedroom window. I continued anyway.

"Trees give us the wood that keeps us warm all winter," I said, trying not to sound pedantic.

"Uh, huh."

"Trees even make the air we breathe." She finally returned my look, evidently ready to join me back here on terra firma. I was preparing to go on about how trees kept the rain from washing topsoil away when she asked me if I wanted to go out and play in her sandbox.

Thinking back on this little lesson, I wonder if perhaps I'd missed an opportunity to share with her the sheer beauty of the lush mid-June landscape, and the patterns of leaves as they moved in the afternoon breeze. It is important for us grown-ups to retain this innocent appreciation of the bounty and beauty of nature for our mental and spiritual well-being.

As grown-ups though, we all carry the burden of knowledge: the cause-and-effect relationship we have with the world we live in. I would love to share the beliefs of those people who espouse the "Gaia" theory: that our planet is a living organism with an inherent capacity for self-healing. In fact, I do feel that there is a thread of truth in all such earnest theories. However, I don't believe the Gaia theory can excuse us from taking responsibility for the unprecedented impact that we as a species have on our environment. In the final analysis, we are all responsible for our actions, our lifestyles, and the decisions we make.

You might argue that, if we could only stand back far enough from the Earth, we would realize that it is truly just a huge, single organism — exchanging forms of energy and matter — and that our human actions are just what they should be. Even if that should prove to be the case, I still hope that our efforts to keep from turning our home into an environmental wasteland succeed, so that our children's children don't have to look back on the past as a better time to have been alive.

To be sure, we humans are clever. In the future we will no doubt adapt to whatever our environment becomes. Even now research is under way to see how we can live in a totally man-made environment. To which I say, "No thanks." I would rather try to live sensibly under the same blue sky that's been around for eons.

Woodburning is another activity that's been around for a long time. It has been a force in our long process of becoming civilized. Wood is a fuel that is renewable, but we must treat it as the valuable crop it is and not overharvest it. We really don't have any choice, for if the trees go, Homo sapiens goes with them. However, considering the vast, unutilized potential of biomass fuel from organic waste and unmanaged forests, this energy source can be expected to play a greater role in supplying the world's energy needs.

Wood and biomass aren't appropriate options for everyone. Economics, storage, local availability, and manual stove operation are all factors to be considered. Because of modern lifestyles and wood's manual loading requirement, it is best used as a companion fuel and heat source.

This book is about woodburning. It is a practical, how-to

guide for those who have never heated with wood. It answers the basic questions that come to mind, from loading a stove to dealing with the ashes.

It is also a resource for experienced woodburners who are thinking of upgrading their old stoves, or who have had a chimney fire and want to avoid another such experience. And it is for those who are concerned about the environmental impact of woodburning.

This book is also for heating and building contractors and building code and fire officials — everyone, in short, who is interested in current methods and products in the woodburning industry.

If you don't read any further, but plan to burn wood, please take these three points seriously:

1. Have your chimney and wood stove installation inspected. Updated fire-safety codes and standards more accurately reflect the requirements of modern solid fuel heating equipment.
2. "Burn it hot." Don't load the stove and close the intake air so that the fire smolders. If you cannot see the fire with the stove running, you should see a flame as soon as you open the loading door.
3. Check the connector pipe and chimney for creosote build-up, and clean the entire venting system when there is ¼ inch or more of creosote.

It has been nearly twenty years since the first OPEC oil embargo and the rebirth of coal and wood heating in this country. Yet it remains a relatively new form of residential heating for most of us. I hope that with a little education and background you will find, as I have, that wood heating, once understood and respected, can be a very safe and satisfying way to stay warm in winter.

CHAPTER 1
Why Burn Wood?

Have you ever noticed how people gather around a fireplace in a ski lodge or common room? It's a lot like being with people at the seashore. No one owns the ocean but it's an elemental part of our world, and we gather around it. And so it is with fire. Fire is nature's way of giving us the sun's warmth. Burning wood isn't only about energy independence, resourcefulness, or economics. It's about the hearth and its rightful place in our homes.

Woodburning can be an intelligent and environmentally sound home heating option, whether it is used as a primary or supplemental source of heat. Among the other home heating fuels, wood is the one renewable fuel that can be harvested with one's own labor and a modest investment in equipment. Forested land provides us with storm-damaged trees; trees cleared for development, or roadway and utility maintenance; and standing dead and deadfall timber. Sound woodlot management yields significant firewood from the process of thinning out crooked, non-lumber-grade trees and less desirable species. The byproduct of logging operations leaves firewood from unusable limbs and trees cut for access roads.

In any wooded environment, there is both oxygen production from growing trees and the release of carbon dioxide — the "greenhouse" gas — as dead wood decays. Since these gases are products of a natural cycle, we may as well use them to heat our homes, as long as our woodburning is done responsibly and in harmony with the environment.

From a geopolitical perspective, the woodburner can also derive some satisfaction from the thought that Btus created from burning wood implicitly reduce the risks associated with our society's insatiable thirst for oil and other fossil fuels — risks as far-reaching and dangerous as "Operation Desert Storm" or the Exxon *Valdez* incident.

◆

1

A HISTORICAL PERSPECTIVE

Even a thousand years ago, woodburning Europeans were concerned about fuel efficiency. Urban populations made fire safety a social concern, and a ready supply of firewood was a valued commodity. With wood, the material almost exclusively used for cooking, heating, and building, the per capita consumption was significant. Aside from these domestic uses, the demand for wood by industry for foundries, bakeries, glassworks, and the like, also took its toll on the forests.

In addition to wood's popularity and usefulness, we should remember that the period between 1550 and 1850, is now sometimes referred to as the "Little Ice Age." During these years Europe was experiencing its own energy crisis, long before heating oil was even known.

Together, all of these factors — increasing demand, dwindling supplies, and a severe climatic change — led to the quest for efficient wood heating.

The Ageless Significance of Fire

As "keepers of the fire," we have had an intimate relationship with fire since our beginnings as a species. In fact, the word *focus* is derived from the Latin word meaning "hearth." The French word *foyer* means "fireplace"; figuratively it also means "home." Even today, fire is still the focal point of our living rooms.

Alexander Marschak wrote in *The Roots of Civilization* that fire "must be tended; it needs a home and place out of the great winds, the heavy rains, the deepest snows; it must be constantly fed." Fire helped to unite people with a single purpose, and feeding it undoubtedly became a task of coordination and cooperation. Camp sites were established in proximity to wood and had to be moved as nearby supplies became exhausted. The Sioux treated fire with care, lest it become dangerous. Fire is the symbol of Light or the visible manifestation of God according to Zoroastrian scripture. The Egyptians knew fire by many names: The Useful One, The Executioner, The Living One, The Angry One, The Beautiful One, The Withering One. The Hawaiian island of Maui is named for the hero who brought back fire from a volcano—home of Mahuika, the fire god. In Greek mythology,

Prometheus brought fire to the people of the Greek island of Symni.

The importance of fire spawned the tradition of the eternal flame — the fire that never dies. In early times women kept the fire, as did the Vestal Virgins at their temple in ancient Rome. The Olympic torch and the eternal flame at Arlington National Cemetery bear witness to fire's continued symbolic role today. A Zoroastrian temple is reported to have had a fire burning continuously for 2,500 years.

Some Native Americans revived the tradition of the Ghost Dance, which included rubbing sticks together to make fire. They refused to adopt the flint and steel brought by the white man. Instead they always kept a fire burning in their lodges as a symbol of eternal life and a sign that they were attentive to the eternal order of things.

These concerns continue today as wood heating and biomass (plant-derived fuels) energy production play a vital role in the mix of global energy sources. Fire also comes to us, as one contemporary writer put it,

> *". . . over wires from a monster hearth at a utility, of which we know little or nothing, and over which we have no real control. Just possibly, in this age of nuclear fires, it is time to regain some control over an element central to our lives, and to restore some of the attentiveness and respect for fire that even our remote ancestors knew."*
>
> David Lyle, *The Book of Masonry Stoves*. Acton, Massachusetts: Brick House Publishing, 1983, p. 16.

Sociologists talk about modern man's sense of alienation, which dates from about the time we began to put our age-old heat source in the basement. With the advent of the furnace, we may also have forsaken the value of self-determination.

Occasionally, people tell me how happily they gave up the drudgery of woodburning when the price of oil dropped. I'm in total sympathy. Trying to insert a woodburning routine into a modern lifestyle, especially when the initial impetus was economic, can be trying at best. Add to that an initial load of wet wood, a chimney with a poor draft, and some back pain from hauling wood. Now you have a disenchanted woodburner!

THE CHOICE OF WOOD

So why burn wood? There are probably as many answers to this question as there are woodburners. Most people would agree that from burning wood they derive personal satisfaction, economic benefits and energy independence.

Economics

A friend of mine said that here in New England we have our own oil wells. Just gaze upon the countryside! There is no question that there is a considerable untapped potential for fuel wood in our forests. The increased demand in recent years has made it more feasible for logging operators to recover tree tops for sale as firewood and to develop more efficient ways of harvesting and processing trees that are not of lumber grade. The key to maintaining our valuable wood resource is conscientious forest management and tree planting programs.

Sample Cost Analysis

This cost analysis makes certain assumptions about fuel prices. The current price for firewood, cut, split, and delivered, is today between $90 and $100 per 128-cubic-foot cord. If an average cord of wood containing 22.5 million Btus of heat is consumed in an EPA-certified stove with an overall efficiency rating of 70 percent, wood costs $6.35 per million Btu of heat delivered to the living space.

No. 2 heating oil, on the other hand, sells for about $1.25 per gallon. With a heat content of 19,000 Btus/gallon, a state-of-the-art oil burner delivers 112,000 Btus of heat for each gallon of oil at a cost of $11.16 per million Btus.

If you purchase natural gas for $0.90 per therm (a **therm** is 100,000 Btus of fuel energy), a high-efficiency condensing furnace might produce heat at a cost of $8.10 per million Btu. (With central heating, the actual amount of heat delivered to the living space also depends on the percentage lost on the way from the furnace to the radiators or convectors. This then, adds to the cost of the fuel if the piping or ducting loses heat to space that you don't want or need to heat.)

◆

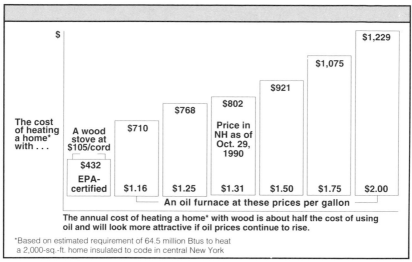

The cost of heating a home* with . . .

	A wood stove at $105/cord	$710	$768	Price in NH as of Oct. 29, 1990	$921	$1,075	$1,229
	$432 EPA-certified	$1.16	$1.25	$802 $1.31	$1.50	$1.75	$2.00

$

An oil furnace at these prices per gallon

The annual cost of heating a home* with wood is about half the cost of using oil and will look more attractive if oil prices continue to rise.

*Based on estimated requirement of 64.5 million Btus to heat a 2,000-sq.-ft. home insulated to code in central New York

◆ Figure 1-1. *Home heating costs. Wood vs. oil at a range of prices.*   Corning, Inc.

In the above comparison, wood is the cheapest fuel. The analysis, however, isn't complete until the initial costs of a certified stove and perhaps a prefabricated chimney are factored in. And, if the wood-heating appliance supplies only half of the home's heating requirement, the payback period for the installation is doubled.

Will the stacking and hauling of firewood, the extra cleanup, the ash removal, and stove loading be figured at your regular job's rate of pay? If so, your fuel savings will probably be offset by the labor costs you attach to your woodburning chores. However, if you have more time than money, you shouldn't consider these chores as added cost. In fact, wood heating can offer even greater savings in terms of cash outlay if you buy wood in log lengths and cut and split it yourself.

For those of you who follow the route to woodburning out of economic necessity, don't take shortcuts on your installation or on maintenance! The ongoing costs associated with woodburning include: chimney cleaning, stovepipe and gasket replacement, stove paint or polish, and perhaps a catalytic combustor if your stove uses that technology.

Personal Satisfaction

New woodburners should ask themselves if the time it takes to do the "wood routine" can become a form of rewarding therapy or even meditation. I find that the attitude one cultivates toward the chores associated with woodburning, determines the amount of satisfaction one derives. The Sufi mystic Pir-o-Murshid Hazrat Inayat Khan says, "For every loss there is a gain, and for every gain there is a loss in life." With this thought in mind, I see my wood chores as the dues I pay for the satisfaction of providing my own heat. Have you ever climbed a peak and experienced the thrill of taking in the breathtaking expanse? Is not the view always worth the climb? This is the kind of satisfaction I enjoy as a woodburner.

Burning wood also helps me take a more positive attitude toward the onset of winter. With great empathy I watch the squirrel's nut-gathering activities every autumn as I go about my wood gathering and splitting; both of us are united in preparing for winter.

Emergency Heat Source

We sometimes forget just how dependent on electricity we are. Until there's a power outage. In western Massachusetts we had a freak snowstorm one October. Many leaves remained on the branches to catch 14 inches of wet, heavy snow, and the trees suffered massive damage.

Although the power was out for less than a day, we were very grateful for our parlor stove. It kept us warm and cooked our dinner. This leads me to an aspect of woodburning that for some people is the most important. Woodburning means, to a greater or lesser extent, energy independence.

WOODBURNING IN THE U.S. SINCE 1973

A mass woodburning experiment started in response to the Arab Oil Embargo of 1973. Stove manufacturers couldn't keep up with the demand. As a result, the quality of their products was variable and many designs were inferior. Do-it-yourself stove installations were not inspected. Stove selection was done with a "bigger is better" attitude, which resulted in excessive amounts of hazardous creosote in the chimney and a rise in loss of property and lives from house fires. On cold, still evenings in the suburbs when the smoke hung heavy in the air, the odor was disagreeable, unlike that of an open campfire. These fires were smoldering, discharging unburned, polluting gases and particulate matter which fouled the air. High-elevation communities where thermal inversions are prevalent suffer the most from these unhealthy emissions. Eventually, widespread woodburning brought the issue of air quality to the fore.

The dangers of chimney fires led woodburners to become more sophisticated about the need to burn seasoned firewood and to burn with enough combustion air to maintain a vigorous fire in the appliance and not in the chimney. This knowledge is vital today. Not only is clean combustion necessary to reduce the risk of chimney fires, but it is essential for completing the carbon dioxide cycle without taxing our environment in the process.

As long as the firing rate is manually controlled by the operator, clean, fuel-efficient woodburning can be compromised; it is physically impossible to achieve over-long burn times on a load of fuel without fouling both the chimney and the environment. The good news is that EPA certification has ushered in a new generation of stoves which, *when operated according to the manufacturer's instructions*, allow residential wood heating to be done with minimal impact on the environment. These appliances have undergone extensive research and development that have created a new "clean burn technology." These stoves aren't only a little better than the old ones; field testing has shown a five- to ten-fold reduction in emissions.

In today's ever-shrinking world each of us has a responsibility to burn cleanly. In areas of the country where the airshed is particularly sensitive, this is imperative, or the right to burn wood could be taken from us.

Environmentally, both wood and pellets (made from renewable and recyclable materials) belong in the mix of home heating options. These are relatively new and small energy industries. They need our support to compete with the established nuclear and fossil fuel giants. Today, more than ever before, it is critical for us as energy consumers to make informed, intelligent, and conscientious decisions.

CHAPTER 2
Wood: A Renewable Energy Resource

In meeting our future energy needs, geothermal power, photovoltaic cells, solar collectors, wind systems, hydropower, wood, and biomass may play a critical role as renewable energy sources.

NUCLEAR POWER

Nuclear power, however, is cited by some policy makers as an ideal alternative to fossil fuels. But we need to ask some hard questions about the potential risks of nuclear power to ourselves and to the environment. Is the government applying the same safety standards to the nuclear industry as it applies to other energy providers? Is the public being asked to assume the excessive risks and hidden costs (such as plant decommissioning and radioactive waste storage)? Could the industry stay in business without being underwritten by the government?

A study by Public Citizen, a research and advocacy organization, concluded that "further investments in nuclear power ... coupled with [its] environmental and safety shortcomings and its long construction time eliminate nuclear power as a credible option for reducing carbon-dioxide emissions from coal- and oil-fired electrical generating plants. On the other hand, investments in energy efficiency improvements, conservation, renewable energy, and selected natural gas technologies would be far less expensive and environmentally safer. In addition, they would yield results in a shorter time frame than nuclear power development."

GROWING UP WITH TECHNOLOGY

The quality of life for all living things on this planet is deteriorating. This is a sad and sobering fact, but one that we, as the species most responsible, must acknowledge. If we are to survive, we will have to adjust some of the fundamental ways in which we live. Our lifestyle is vastly different from that of our ancestors. In some ways it has been greatly improved. We certainly live at a faster pace, and many mundane tasks of daily life have become much easier. But now that the fascination, novelty, and glamour of technology have worn off, we can see the negative environmental impact of conspicuous energy consumption. We need to convince our legislators that certain goods and services, even though they are created in the name of "jobs" or "the economy," are too costly to the environment and further deplete our rapidly diminishing natural resources. We have become dependent on cheap, readily available fossil fuels. Once we recognize this addiction, we can look for methods that employ appropriate technologies to maintain our standard of living. An **appropriate** technology is one that we can sustain without a net degradation of the planet. Countries that pay more for fossil fuel and those in colder climates already provide directions and solutions for less energy-consumptive lifestyles.

Appropriate Technology

The purpose of this book is to recognize that, in regions with plenty of trees, clean combustion woodburning is an appropriate technology for home heating. In regions of this country where sensitive airsheds have been polluted by poorly operated wood stoves, there must be a process of re-education. In the early days we simply "knew not what we were doing." Early woodburners bought stoves which were too large, and produced sufficient heat from smoldering wood (air-starved fires set for long burn cycles). This permitted longer cycles between refueling, but fouled the air and reduced fuel efficiency in the process. In these regions, regulations to restrict woodburning have been a natural and understandable reaction. But in some cases, air quality regulations have "thrown the baby out with the bath water." They have focused not on emissions but on woodburning itself.

If the woodburning industry were as well-funded as the National Rifle Association, it might have mounted a similar campaign using the slogan, "Wood Stoves Don't Pollute. People Pollute." Instead, the industry was forced to bear the cost of research and development to meet EPA standards, to consolidate (or go out of business), and to ride out the storm. The "high-tech" wood stoves that resulted from the shake-up of the woodburning industry are both user- and environment-friendly.

This latest generation of wood stoves meets Phase II of EPA's regulations. Emissions have been reduced by an average of 75 percent, and fuel efficiency has improved from 20 to 40 percent. Under tremendous pressure from federal and state regulators, the wood stove industry has met a formidable challenge.

ENERGY PLANNING

Making conscious choices about the products we buy and the way we live is a big first step. If a free market economy is to survive as a way to exchange goods and services, the system must make environmental impact an integral part of doing business.

It is encouraging to see some major corporations changing to more ecologically sound packaging policies. It is also a hopeful sign that we are beginning to do large-scale recycling, re-using, and reducing the amount of waste we create, even if the high cost of disposal has been the driving force.

As the nation with the largest per capita consumption of natural resources and energy, we have a responsibility to our children and to the rest of the planet to lead the way in energy planning. That means promoting individual and corporate lifestyles consistent with long-range estimates of energy consumption. The simple, supply-side approach to this challenge is inadequate, because proportionally greater levels of energy production and consumption, from whatever source, will only exacerbate global warming. I'm not against supply-side economics, as long as the *cost to the environment* is included in the equation. If we proceed from incomplete equations, we are certain to have incomplete solutions.

For 20 years the Japanese have dominated the automobile industry — with gas-stingy cars. Why do we still lack an energy policy that requires a strong commitment to greater fuel efficiency? If the price we pay for gasoline included the cost to the environment, we would be demanding fuel-efficient cars. Since energy is Big Business at its biggest, it is crucial that this new energy policy be drafted according to sound ecological principles. We as citizens need to be aware of the issues involved if we are to promise our grandchildren a world that they will be able to enjoy and maintain. Grassroots education and involvement are essential.

Corporations aren't the enemy. Corporations are made up of people; to survive and prosper, we all need a healthy planet. We need to be more than consumers in this process. We must, even by our simple choices, be co-creators of the goods and services we buy. Beyond that, we should require our legislators to look at the long-term, total picture when drafting future energy policy.

Renewables is a buzzword among many energy policy makers. Research and development for renewables has been slow, and the industry is largely decentralized, but renewable energy sources will play an ever-increasing role in energy production. Currently, renewable energy technologies account for 8 percent of the nation's total energy supply. By the year 2000, with only limited backing from the government, that figure could double. Biomass (primarily wood) accounted for 3 percent of U.S. energy consumption in 1980 and is expected to reach 10 percent by the end of the century.

The graph to the left shows one projection of our increasing reliance on renewable sources of energy for the future. You may wonder how any projection for energy

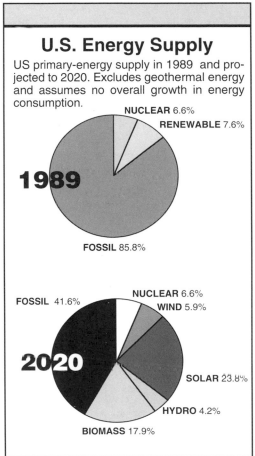

U.S. Energy Supply

US primary-energy supply in 1989 and projected to 2020. Excludes geothermal energy and assumes no overall growth in energy consumption.

1989
NUCLEAR 6.6%
RENEWABLE 7.6%
FOSSIL 85.8%

2020
FOSSIL 41.6%
NUCLEAR 6.6%
WIND 5.9%
SOLAR 23.8%
HYDRO 4.2%
BIOMASS 17.9%

◆ Figure 2-1   *Coal Energy (1900)*, Union of Concerned Scientists sources in the year 2020 could assume no overall growth in consumption. However, the aggressive adoption of conservation legislation alone could achieve a leveled growth.

Biomass Energy Crops

Increasingly, non-lumber-grade timber and the by-products of harvesting sawlogs are being chipped for fuel. As of 1989, there were over 400 wood-fired power plants in Northeast businesses, industries, hospitals, and apartment buildings. Maine alone generates 453 megawatts of wood-fired electricity and has plans to generate another 60 Mw.

Recycled Wood Wastes

Research conducted under the Northeast Regional Biomass Program (NRBP) indicates that "five years from now the generation of electricity from wood wastes should be commonplace throughout the country."

In 1987, Americans disposed of 35 to 40 million tons of woody materials from demolished buildings, land clearing, and other industrial and commercial activities. As landfill space becomes increasingly scarce — and expensive — a market for woody waste as a fuel for commerical energy production will emerge as well as related businesses for handling, processing, and utilizing this growing resource.

Wood waste contains contaminants, such as paint, resins, and preservatives, which may produce air pollutants when burned. The current research being conducted by NRBP at laboratories and select field boiler sites in Canada and the U.S. seeks to identify combustion system operation parameters and air pollution control technologies that can minimize the emissions from wood waste combustion.

In addition to the usefulness of biomass fuels as potential power sources for industries and institutions, they can also be pelletized for uniformity. This pelletized fuel processed and produced from a variety of regional sources not only helps to re-use and recycle current waste products, but can provide clean and efficient home heating.

Municipalities now give careful consideration to another potential energy source — solid wastes. Energy production from municipal wastes in resource recovery and anerobic digestion facilities is emerging as a major solid waste strategy. Methane gas from landfills is also being tapped.

WOODBURNING AND GLOBAL WARMING

The coming crisis of global warming, according to a study by Public Citizen, "necessitates solutions that address the sources of greenhouse emissions, that measures be implemented in a relatively short time frame, and that the strategies employed entail costs (both economic and environmental) which the U.S. is able and willing to pay."

At a minimum, more than two-thirds (68 percent) of the carbon dioxide produced by the combustion of coal and oil for generating electricity as well as that used in homes, businesses, and industry could be eliminated by the year 2000 through modest investments in energy efficiency, renewable energy, and selected natural gas technologies. (A 50 percent reduction in carbon dioxide emissions is often cited as necessary to ameliorate the trend toward global warming.)

> *"The potential for utilizing biomass resources to address the global climate change crisis is twofold. First, biomass combustion — especially wood — can displace coal and oil, both of which emit carbon dioxide into the atmosphere in greater quantities per unit of energy produced. Second, where appropriate, reforestation practices and prudent forestry management policies can increase forest growth, which in turn increases the region's [planet's] carbon-fixing capacity."*
>
> Northeast Regional Biomass Program Mission,
> Accomplishments Prospects, 1991

In the context of global warming, forests are referred to as carbon dioxide "sinks." The U.S. Forest Service estimates that our forests could produce 16 billion cubic feet more wood. These additional trees would consume 500 million tons of atmospheric CO_2 annually. In addition, the management of these forests would yield harvests of fuel wood, which would release CO_2 whether the wood rots in the forest or is consumed in a fire.

Nature provides a nice balance in the atmosphere of the gases that are essential to life on our planet. Animals, including humans, require oxygen to sustain life. In the process of converting food into energy, we exhale carbon dioxide. Plants on the other hand, utilize this same gas in their growth process. They emit oxygen into the atmosphere as they grow. Plant and animal life are mutually supportive.

Greenhouse Gases

"Without carbon dioxide in the atmosphere, life as we know it would be impossible," according to Elmer Robinson, director of the Mauna Loa observatory in Hawaii. Carbon dioxide levels have been recorded at that observatory since 1958. Researchers have found during these 34 years that the level of CO_2 has risen steadily from 315 parts per million (ppm) to more than 355 ppm. Robinson predicts that by the middle of the next century, the CO_2 level will reach 550 to 600 ppm at its current rate of increase. Climatologists are busily creating computer models to show what the effects of an anticipated global warming of 3° to 9°F. would mean. Of course, human behavior adds a complicating "wild card" to the scenario. The experts are in general agreement that the earth is in a warming trend and that this trend will continue. Many respected scholars from all over the world have said that global warming is the most serious threat that we as a species have to face.

The increasing concentration of atmospheric CO_2 is a direct result of burning ever greater amounts of fossil fuels — gasoline, natural gas, and coal, all of which left the carbon cycle long ago. Carbon dioxide is not, however, the only greenhouse gas. Methane from plant and animal decomposition is increasing even faster than CO_2, and molecule for molecule methane has 20 to 30 times the greenhouse effect. Nitrogen gases — from fertilizers, cars, and factories — is 200 times as heat-absorbing as CO_2. Chlorofluorocarbons (CFCs) from refrigerators, air conditioners, and aerosol propellants can be 16,000 times more heat-absorbing than CO_2 and comprise as much as 20 percent of man-made contributions to global warming. These other gases from human activity are already doubling the warming potential of CO_2 alone.

Three courses of action emerge from these findings:

1. Continued support for research at regional, national, and international levels to increase global awareness and cooperation.

2. Active promotion of technologies and fuels that will reduce the addition of greenhouse gases to the atmosphere. Or, in the words of one article, "Rapidly adopting energy efficiency measures and substituting renewable biomass resources for fossil fuels is a reasonable course because they already make economic and environmental sense." (*Biologue*, Dec./Jan. 1988–89.)

3. Learning to adapt to a changing environment. This means developing drought-resistant crop strains, irrigation methods, and alternative cooling strategies. Adaptation goes on daily in nature; we must learn to do it as well.

WHAT ABOUT THE FORESTS?

Proper forest management is essential if we expect to maintain a habitable planet. The enormous destruction of the Amazon rainforest is a sad example of natural resource abuse and ecological disregard in the name of short-term economic benefit. Clearly, the costs to the environment were not factored into the equation.

In the same vein, I would argue that our "old growth" forests are not a renewable resource — not unless we harvest them at a slow enough rate to have at least the same number of 300-year-old trees as we now have in the West Coast of the U.S. and in Canada.

There were old growth forests in New England when the Pilgrims arrived. They were cleared or cut for ship masts and timber-frame buildings. But they were cut with much human effort and for more appropriate uses than fast food wrappers and third-class mail. Today the majority of our forests are privately owned by the big lumber companies. Environmentalists are concerned that decisions regarding this valuable resource are being made in the interests of profitable business at the expense of the long-term well-being of these ecosystems. Again, there is a need to look at "the complete equation."

◆

Private groups like the Nature Conservancy purchase particularly sensitive ecosystems and scenic landscapes for protection against development. Also, some states buy conservation easements from farmers and other individuals. These easements preserve agricultural lands whose scenic beauty encourages tourism in the region. Vermont has a statute that declares all land above 2000 feet part of the Green Mountain National Forest and subject to strict requirements for private use.

Massachusetts land owners can utilize Chapter 61 to gain forest management guidelines from state foresters, in addition to a lower real estate tax rate if they own sufficient land. In return, landowners follow a management plan and development restrictions.

However, the growing demand for wood products puts forest management legislation under economic and political stress. Political policy and public vigilance are required to ensure that forests are renewed as they are used.

Even here in New England where trees grow like weeds, reforestation programs are essential to insure a future supply of mature trees for lumber.

"There are 55 million acres of commercial forestlands in the eleven northeastern states. Surplus growth in these forests has the capacity to provide annually two to four times the volume of wood fuels than what is currently utilized, without jeopardizing the Northeast's vigorous pulp, paper, and wood products industries.

"This energy harvest can be accomplished without harm to forestlands. If sound forest management practices are used to keep residual stand damage to a minimum, wood fuel harvesting can generate positive impacts on the region's forests. Harvesting low-quality, previously unmerchantable wood in thinning operations improves conditions for the growth of the higher-quality trees which remain. Vigorous reforestation can make wood fuel resources entirely renewable as well as contribute to reducing atmospheric carbon dioxide."

Coalition of Northeastern Governors' Policy Research Center, Inc.,
Northeast Regional Biomass Program, March 1991. Washington, D.C.

The U.S. Forest Service advises that approximately one cord of firewood can be harvested from one acre of forest in the course of forest management. After land has been lumbered, modern machinery can chip the tree branches into fuel instead of leaving them to rot on the forest floor.

WOOD HARVESTING

Wood harvesting techniques that were once widely employed have long since been forgotten. But if we increasingly turn to wood for heat, coppicing and pollarding could be important techniques for ensuring a renewable fuel supply.

Coppicing is encouraging tree shoots from the stump of a harvested tree. A benefit of this practice is the root structure of the original tree prevents erosion that usually accompanies modern clear-cutting practices.

Since the new shoots may be easily eaten by livestock and wildlife, the tree can be felled at a sufficient height to protect the shoots. This alternative method is called **pollarding**. Because something is left of the original tree, the process is truly renewable.

Figure 2-2. In a coppice (left) trees were cut approximately at ground level. Pollard trees (bottom) were cut well above ground level.

The Book of Masonry Stoves by David Lyle.

17

Chapter 3
Energy Conservation

Satisfying our future energy needs will require not only many different energy sources, but also a sound and environmentally responsible energy policy. This policy should advocate that we: Conserve fuel, burn fuel cleanly and efficiently, maintain a diversity of energy sources, and choose renewable resources over fossil fuels whenever possible.

The Reagan era taught us that conservation meant "freezing in the dark"; in reality, conservation means using energy as efficiently as possible.

Since all forms of energy production have some environmental impact, we should first concentrate on using every Btu that we produce as wisely and efficiently as possible. Between 1973 and 1985, energy efficiency reduced U.S. consumption per unit of gross national product by 28 percent (this represents 29 quadrillion Btus — or quads — compared to total energy use of 80 quads in the U.S. in 1987), while the economy grew by 35 percent. These energy efficiency improvements now save the United States $160 billion per year. In addition, substantially greater savings are possible with more favorable political support.

The success of conservation has also encouraged the public utilities to manage their power supplies. But our ever-growing demand for energy may force us to look at human activities in terms of their appropriateness as energy users. We may even have to prohibit needless uses of energy, and demand that every energy unit produced be used in the most efficient way possible.

Wood heat has limits as well, but by insulating and tightening up your house you can significantly reduce the amount of heat you have to produce.

Active versus Passive Solar Heating

Passive solar refers to the practice of installing a large area of glass on the south side(s) of a house. Objects exposed to the greater sunlight absorb the radiant heat energy and in turn raise the inside temperature. **Active solar systems** employ mechanical means to move and store heat. Large areas of (usually sloping) glazing are required to heat either air or water. Fans and pumps then move the heated medium to a storage area for use as needed.

Passive solar heating is more cost-effective than active systems in the Northeast because of the average yearly amount of sun. Sunspaces that employ an insulated masonry floor and/or masonry Trombe wall will maximize the storage capability of passive solar heat gain. The thermosiphoning air panels (TAPs), Trombe walls, and window greenhouses are all passive solar heating strategies that work indirectly — heating and circulating warm air.

KEEPING HEAT INSIDE THE HOME

I was once called in to clean the chimney and assess a wood heating system for a client who lived on an exposed hilltop in the Berkshires. The nineteenth-century Cape had several windows without "storms," and the building lacked insulation. The occupants heated their 1000-square-foot home with a converted coal furnace. The furnace was in a drafty basement, and the heat reached the living area through uninsulated hot air ducts. The owner told me that the basement was the warmest place in the house and that he spent most of his time either "keeping the fire" or securing wood for it. They burned twelve to fourteen cords per winter — at least twice what should have been needed.

I cite the above example to illustrate the ramifications involved when energy conservation and efficiency principles are not employed. I felt sorry for the homeowner, whose situation reflected a difficult financial situation that kept him bound to a very labor-intensive heating regimen. If we look at the **scale** of impact this example gives us applied to automobiles, for instance, we can begin to get a grasp of the magnitude of the oil exploration, drilling, transportation, and consumption **eliminated** by driving more fuel efficient cars.

To effectively heat with wood, first minimize the home heat load. The **heat load** of a house is measured in Btus/hr and is the heating requirement necessary to maintain 65° to 68°F. temperatures during the coldest weather. Insulating, caulking, and weatherstripping your home will dramatically decrease the house's heat load. If you ignore basic home conservation strategies, you will be heating the outdoors.

Cutting Heat Loss

There are a number of cost-effective measures that reduce heat loss in a home. The back of the hand is sensitive to cold air and can be used as an infiltration gauge. **Infiltration** occurs when cold air leaks in; inside air leaks out. When this occurs, the heating appliance must make up the difference.

It doesn't take long to identify many leaky places around doors and windows. These can be weatherized at very little expense.

1. Weatherstrip doors and install a door sweep along the bottom edge.
2. Weatherstrip or seal operable windows for the winter with a removable rope caulk.
3. Remove or cover window air conditioners. If the unit is mounted permanently, cover the inside *and* outside with a polyethylene or with a manufacturer's cover.
4. Caulk the cracks and gaps where the wooden house sill meets the foundation, around chimneys, where dryer vents and fan covers pass through an exterior wall, where pipes and telephone wires enter the house, and in any place outside where two different materials meet.
5. On the house exterior walls, install switch and outlet gaskets. Remember to turn off the electricity to the outlets or switches before you install the gaskets and be sure to use only UL-approved products.
6. Seal air leaks into the attic. If the attic is uninsulated, the ceiling below forms the top of the building envelope. Be sure to seal around hatchways and attic doors. Gaps around

◆

chimneys should be stuffed with unfaced fiberglass batting.

7. Block off unused fireplaces. If the damper doesn't seal tightly, clean the surfaces of the damper frame and damper. Then use a foil tape to seal it. It may be easier to close off or seal the opening of the fireplace itself.

8. Weatherstrip the garage door if the garage is attached to the house and acts as a buffer between the heated space and the outdoors. Reducing the air infiltration into the garage will reduce heat transfer through the common wall or ceiling. Garage door weatherstripping tacks to the bottom of the door, and is available at most local hardware stores.

Insulating Tips

The following steps will reduce the heat load of your house and also be cost-effective.

1. Insulate the domestic hot water heater. Insulation kits make the job much simpler and should be used.

2. Insulate the pipes from the hot water heater and furnace. The pipe insulation should fit snugly and is available at hardware stores.

3. Insulate hot air ducts. Use vinyl (preferred) or foil-backed fiberglass duct insulation with a minimum 1½-inch thickness and an R-value of at least 5.4. This insulation should fit snugly.

4. Insulate the space between joists in floors above an unheated space. Use 6-inch-thick, R-19, foil-faced fiberglass or mineral wool or the equivalent. If the unheated space has a ceiling, blow a loose fill insulation into the cavity between the ceiling and the floor above. Use only materials that meet federal fire and safety standards. If cellulose is used, the fire retardant should be boron-based.

5. Insulate crawl spaces if the area is adjacent to a heated basement with excess heat. The insulation should run from the band joist down the wall and out onto the ground. Use R-19 blanket insulation over 4 or 6 mil polyethylene sheeting. If the ground level of the space is damp, or if the space is separate from a heated basement, floor insulation may be more appropriate. (If this is the case, refer to Step #4 above.)

6. Insulate the slab. For homes built on a slab this entails digging down around the perimeter to a depth of at least two feet and using polystyrene rigid insulation with a minimum R-10 rating. Exposed insulation should be stuccoed to prevent deterioration from sunlight and physical abuse.
7. Insulate attic with either loose fill or blanket insulation. The insulation should be R-30 where space allows. Keep the insulation away from soffit vents and heat-producing sources such as light fixtures. Ventilation must be provided to reduce the build-up of moisture and heat in an insulated attic. Some combination of gable, roof, ridge, turbine, and soffit vents must be installed. If no vapor barrier exists, use the ratio of 1 square foot of net free vent area for each 150 square feet of attic floor area. If a vapor barrier exists, 1 square foot of open vent area for each 300 square feet of attic floor area is adequate. Ventilation is most effective when half of the vents are located as high in the attic as possible, and the other half toward the bottom of the attic. Vapor barriers must face the living space. Bathroom fans should *not* vent directly into the attic; they can cause moisture build-up.

The following measures are more expensive and therefore have longer payback periods. Nevertheless they are worthwhile.
1. Insulate walls. To check for wall insulation, turn off the power. Remove an outlet or switch plate on an outside wall. Shine a flashlight into the space between the electric box and the wall. If there is no insulation, loose fill can be blown in from either the exterior or interior side of the walls. Consult an insulating contractor.
2. Insulate windows. Insulation is available in a variety of shutters, shades, and panels. Be sure materials are flame-retardant, moisture-resistant, and durable.

HEATING SYSTEM ASSESSMENT

Now that the house is tighter, you may want to consider installing a new boiler (if you have a hot water system) or a new furnace (if you have a hot air system). A new heating system may be more cost-effective than you think — assuming that you use it for most of your heating needs.

If your current unit was converted from coal burning, a new one may be a particularly wise investment. By tightening up your living space, you will have reduced the heating requirements on which the current system is based. An oversized heating system is wasteful for several reasons.

Firstly, the system will "off-cycle" more frequently, which means an increase in "standby" losses (heat drawn through the system and up the flue when the unit is not firing). Secondly, by off-cycling more frequently, the oversized unit permits the flue to cool down, which *increases* the risk of condensation of corrosive flue gases. This causes masonry chimneys and metal flues to deteriorate over time. Damage to the flue increases the risk of blockage and the spillage of flue gases.

Studies indicate that the average heating system in the U.S. is 2.3 times too large! Using a conservative estimate of 5 percent for oversized gas appliances (up to 10 percent for oil-fired equipment), the savings from accurate sizing are substantial. The correct heat load for your house can be calculated using the following chart. When you know the heat load of the building, you can size the boiler or furnace correctly.

If you have a large, ominous-looking boiler, it was designed to burn coal and probably runs at less than 75 percent efficiency. Even an early oil-fired unit with a new, retention head "gun" and smaller nozzle usually runs at less than 80 percent efficiency. Replacement with an appropriately sized boiler that incorporates boiler purging will boost your system's Annual Fuel Utilization Efficiency (AFUE) rating to 87 percent.

AFUE: Annual Fuel Utilization Efficiency. This is a rating used to compare heating system efficiencies by dividing the amount of heat delivered to the space by the heat content of the fuel. This is a conservative percentage taking into account heat losses from the distribution system, start up and standby losses, and a heating season average.

Design Heat Load Worksheet

1. Client name: _____Jones_____

2. Client address: _____Boston, MA_____

_____

3. Client telephone:_____

4. General dwelling description: _____wood frame 36' x 25';_____
   _____2" x 6" walls; crawl space; 1800 sq. ft.;_____
   _____two-story_____

5. Outside design temp. (ODT), 97.5%_____9°_____

6. Volume of dwelling above grade: _____14,400_____

*7. Average winter air changers per hour (ac/h): _____1.2_____
   *See Figure 3-2.

8. Design temp. difference (DTD) = Dwelling temp. − ODT = 61

Transmission						
Surface	Area (sq.ft.)	+	R-Value	=	Btu/°F. hr	
walls	1814		19		95.5	
floor	900		19		47.4	
windows	220		1.8		122.2	
ceiling	900		38		23.7	
doors	40		5		8.0	
0.02 x volume x ac/h = 0.02 x 14,400 x 1.2 =					345.6	
Grand total = heat loss coefficient (HLC)					642.4	
➡ Design heat load = HLC x DTD					39,186.4	

◆ Figure 3-1. *The heat-load worksheet is filled out for a sample house in Boston, Massachusett You need to include all the surface areas that enclose the heated, above-grade portion of th dwelling. This form gives a relatively quick but accurate method to compute the load building's heating system will need to meet. A blank form that you can use or photocopy is c p.142 in the Appendix.* Figures 3.1, 3.2, 3.3, and 3.4 fro
The Journal of Light Construction, August, 1990, by Rick Kar

Infiltration Evaluation

Winter Air Changes Per Hour (ac/h)

Floor Area in Sq. Feet	900 or less	900 – 1500	1500 – 2100	over 2100
Best	0.4	0.4	0.3	0.3
Average	1.2	1.0	0.8	0.7
Poor	2.2	1.6	1.2	1.0

For each fireplace add: Best Average Poor
                        0.1   0.2   0.6

Envelope Evaluation

Best: Continuous infiltration barrier, all cracks and penetrations sealed, tested leakage of windows and doors less then 0.25 CFM per running foot of crack, vents and exhaust fans dampered, recessed ceiling lights gasketed or taped, no combustion air required or combustion air from outdoors, no duct leakage.

Average: Plastic vapor barrier, major cracks and penetrations sealed, tested leakage of windows and doors between 0.25 and 0.50 CFM per running foot of crack, electrical fixtures that penetrate the envelope not taped or gasketed. Vents and exhaust fans dampered, combustion air from indoors, intermittent ignition and flue damper, some duct leakage of unconditioned space.

Poor: No infiltration barrier or plastic vapor barrier, no attempt to seal cracks and penetrations, tested leakage of windows and doors greater than 0.50 CFM per running foot of crack, vents and exhaust fans not dampered, combustion air from indoors, standing pilot, no flue damper, considerable duct leakage to unconditioned space.

Fireplace Evaluation

Best: Combustion air from outdoors, tight glass doors and damper.
Average: Combustion air from indoors, tight glass doors or damper.
Poor: Combustion air from indoors, no glass doors or damper.

Note: Allowance for one kitchen and two bathroom exhaust fans, dryer vent, recessed lighting fixtures, pipe and duct penetrations.

Figure 3-2

Boiler purging is a method to capture standby heat losses in the boiler and distribution system. After the thermostat has been satisfied, the circulator pump runs until the system's water temperature has dropped to approximately 105°F. A storage tank then holds this heated water for either domestic or heating use. One such oil-fired unit, made by Energy Kinetics, Inc., is called the "System 2000." If such a unit is 10 percent more efficient than your present system, and accurate system-sizing yields additional efficiency, fuel savings will be substantial with a reasonably short payback period.

Another feature now available for home heating units is **sealed combustion**. As the name implies, combustion air is brought in from outside, usually through the outer walls of the vent which exhausts through the inner pipe. A significant advantage of this option is that by "uncoupling" the furnace from the inside air, furnace back-venting from a fireplace (or vice versa) is no longer a threat. **Back-venting** occurs when another exhausting appliance overcomes the chimney draft. When this happens, combustion by-products are drawn into the living space.

Calculating Your Heating Costs

To figure your expected Annual Fuel Cost, use the following formula:

$$\text{Annual Fuel Cost} = \frac{\text{DHL}}{\text{DTD}} \times \text{HDD} \times .000015 \times \$/\text{MBtu}$$

where:

DHL = design heat load
DTD = design temperature difference
HDD = heating degree days (see Figure 3-3)
$/MBtu = dollars per millions Btus

Figure 3-3 shows the Outside Design Temperature, or the temperature below which the winter temperature will drop only 2.5 percent of the time. In Boston that is 9°F. The design temperature difference (DTD) is the maximum anticipated temperature difference between the inside and outside for a given location. For Boston the DTD is 70 minus 9 or 61 degrees.

Refer to Figure 3-3 to see how many heating degree days (HDD) there are in your area, or better yet, call the local weather bureau for a more accurate HDD figure for your locale. Use Figure 3-4 and a recent fuel bill to compare the cost in $/MBtu of different heating methods. Don't forget to adjust for your particular system's AFUE efficiency.

Assuming that the result of your heat load calculation (from Figure 3-1) tells you that your DHL is 50,000 Btus/hr, you can determine your yearly fuel bill.

If, for example, you live in Boston and have just installed a "Deep Heat" gas furnace with a seasonal efficiency of 95 percent and gas costs $0.90 per therm, your annual fuel costs are:

$$\frac{50,000}{61} \times 5,630 \times .000015 \times \$9.25 = \$640$$

If you have tightened up the house, kept an old unit with an efficiency of 75 percent, and pay $12.50, the annual fuel cost will be:

$$\frac{50,000}{61} \times 5,630 \times .000015 \times \$12.50 = \$865$$

Note that the larger the heat load of the house, the greater the savings achieved by upgrading the boiler. Strict economics may determine that it is more cost-effective to replace the boiler than to replace leaky windows, for instance. If you need help prioritizing and assessing the cost effectiveness of installing energy-efficient building components, call your state Executive Office of Energy Resources (EOER) or your Department of Public Utilities (DPU) for information. Ask if they offer any kind of residental energy audit.

In Massachussetts, the DPU is required to provide energy at "least cost." This least cost provision includes energy conservation as an energy source, which enables public utilities to make money by promoting conservation. Such progressive legislation has resulted in energy surveys upon request by homeowners — surveys that include installation of a range of energy-efficient amenities, including fluorescent light bulbs, water heater wraps, and low-flow shower heads at no up-front cost.

Weather Data for Selected Cities

	Outside Design Temperature (97.5%)	Heating Degree Days
Anchorage, Alaska	-18	10860
Phoenix, Arizona	34	1680
Little Rock, Arkansas	20	3170
San Francisco, California	38	3040
Denver, Colorado	1	6165
Hartford, Connecticut	7	6170
Washington, DC	17	4240
Miami, Florida	48	200
Atlanta, Georgia	22	2990
Boise, Idaho	10	5830
Chicago, Illinois	2	6640
Indianapolis, Indiana	2	5630
Cedar Rapids, Iowa	-5	6600
Lexington, Kentucky	8	4760
Portland, Maine	-1	7570
Boston, Massachusetts	9	5630
Grand Rapids, Michigan	5	6890
Minneapolis, Minnesota	-12	8250
St. Louis, Missouri	6	4900
Cut Bank, Montana	-20	9033
Lincoln, Nebraska	-2	6050
Reno, Nevada	10	6150
Manchester, New Hampshire	-3	7100
Atlantic City, New Jersey	13	4810
Albuquerque, New Mexico	16	4250
Albany, New York	-1	6900
Raleigh, North Carolina	20	3440
Fargo, North Dakota	-18	9250
Cleveland, Ohio	5	6200
Portland, Oregon	23	4635
Pittsburgh, Pennsylvania	5	5850
Pierre, South Dakota	-10	7550
Jackson, Tennessee	16	3350
Houston, Texas	32	1410
Salt Lake City, Utah	8	5990
Burlington, Vermont	-7	8030
Charlottesville, Virginia	18	4220
Spokane, Washington	2	6770
Milwaukee, Wisconsin	-4	7470
Casper, Wyoming	-5	7510

◆ Figure 3-3

Comparing Heating Fuel Costs

Natural Gas @ 75% Eff. in $/Therm
.50 .60 .70 .80 .90 1.00 1.10 1.20 1.30 1.40 1.50 1.60 1.70 1.80 1.90 2.00 2.10

Natural Gas @ 95% Eff. in $/Therm
.60 .70 .80 .90 1.00 1.10 1.20 1.30 1.40 1.50 1.60 1.70 1.80 1.90 2.00 2.10 2.20 2.30 2.40 2.50 2.60 2.70

Fuel Oil @ 85% Eff. in $/Gallon
.70 .90 1.10 1.30 1.50 1.70 1.90 2.10 2.30 2.50 2.70 2.90 3.10 3.30

LP Gas @ 75% Eff. in $/Gallon
.50 .60 .70 .80 .90 1.00 1.10 1.20 1.30 1.40 1.50 1.60 1.70 1.80 1.90 2.00

LP Gas @ 95% Eff. in $/Gallon
.60 .70 .80 .90 1.00 1.10 1.20 1.30 1.40 1.50 1.60 1.70 1.80 1.90 2.00 2.10 2.20 2.30 2.40 2.50

Mixed Hardwood @ 50% Eff. in $/Cord
70 90 110 130 150 170 190 210 230 250 270 290 310 330 350

Electricity @ 100% Eff. in $/kwh
.025 .03 .035 .04 .045 .05 .055 .06 .065 .07 .075 .08 .085 .09 .095 .10

Heating Equivalent Cost in $/MBtu
6 8 10 12 14 16 18 20 22 24 26 28

ASSUMPTIONS

Natural Gas (100,000 Btu/Therm)	#2 Fuel Oil (138,000 Btu/Gallon)	Mixed Hardwood (24 MBtu/Cord)
	LP Gas (93,000 Btu/Gallon)	Electricity (3412 Btu/kwh)

◆ Figure 3.4. *This chart allows you to quickly compare the costs of different heating options. To find the cost of any option in dollars per million Btus ($/MBtu), find the cost of your fuel on the appropriate horizontal line and read down vertically to the chart's bottom line. For example, the vertical line drawn shows that oil at $1.15 per gallon (at 85% efficient) costs a little over $10/MBtus. You can also see that electricity would need to sell for less than 3½¢ per kwh to compete with oil at $1.15/gal.*

Increasing the Comfort Zone

For anyone who heats their home with a single radiating source, the other significant advantage of reducing heat loss (aside from reducing fuel usage) is that it enlarges the **comfort zone**. This is the maximum distance from the heat source at which one can still experience its heating benefit.

One-story ranch homes or long, rambling spaces present their own heating problems. If you install a wood stove in the family room at one end of the house, the bedrooms at the other end may get very chilly. If to keep the bedrooms at 60°F., you need the temperature in the family room to be 80°F., that setting will be uncomfortably hot. As an alternative, install insulated shades on bedroom windows, insulate the floor and band joists (the first-floor perimeter framing), add another R-10 of insulation to the attic floor, and hang a small high-speed fan in the bedroom doorway. You may find that with the family room at 72°F., the bedrooms are at the desired 60°F.

The tighter and better insulated the building envelope, the less the temperature will drop in those areas not adjacent to a heat source.

Where possible, check your insulation. Some types degrade over time or settle, reducing their effectiveness. And fiberglass insulation can easily lose 40 percent of its effective R-value from infiltration and convective losses in the wall cavity. This is not to say that insulation is not worthwhile — it certainly is. The current emphasis on relative R-values, however, can divert attention from other measures that may prove more cost-effective — like upgrading a wood stove or boiler.

Most of us can't do everything to lower our heating bills at once. When looking at your situation you will want to consider what steps will: (1) have the quickest payback; (2) enhance the long term value; (3) reduce maintenance costs on the home.

WHERE TO BEGIN

No matter how you currently heat your home, you can benefit from investments in energy conservation. Start with an Energy Audit (contact your state Department of Public Utilities or Executive Office of Energy Resources). Some programs prioritize your home's energy needs so you can decide which ones to implement first.

After minimizing your current heating requirements, assess the costs and benefits of the range of available heating fuels. Also examine your lifestyle. Be realistic and honest with yourself. Is burning cordwood merely the "least expensive" heating option or does it represent your desire to be more involved in providing for one of your basic needs?

If convenience is a primary concern and forests aren't a part of your regional geography, pellet burning may be for you. Biomass pellets can create heat from recycled renewables, cleanly, safely, and with minimum attention. They also offer the most environmentally responsible central heating option.

Masonry heaters offer unique benefits for wood heating. While they require a more substantial initial investment, they offer long-time value. Masonry heating is the oldest way of warming and remains unsurpassed in energy efficiency. Recent emissions test results from Omni Labs have led Washington state to include masonry heaters in the "EPA Certified" classification under their strict air quality program.

Chapter 4
Choosing a Heater

When the price of oil first shot up in response to the 1973 oil embargo, entrepreneurial wood stove manufacturers sprang up. Some designs were faulty and quality of workmanship varied greatly, not only among the different stovemakers but between stoves. The new EPA certification ensures that the current wood stoves have been independently tested for clean burning performance. (See Chapter 5 for a discussion of EPA-certified wood stoves.) The regulations also provide for on site, quality assurance testing. This is good for the consumer because you will be satisfying your heating needs with minimum impact on the environment. Also the safety margin has been increased (contingent on use according to the owner's manual and regular professional maintenance); there is a reduced chance of chimney fires and a reduced health risk from chimney stack emissions. You can also be confident that your unit will perform as well as the unit that was tested in the laboratory. Although the cheaper certified stoves now retail for about $700, don't expect to get the same quality of workmanship you would in a stove retailing for twice as much.

Buy your stove from a reputable stove dealer. You want to know that the seller will be responsive to any problems you may have.

WHAT TO LOOK FOR

Look at the loading door mechanism to see if it will endure long, hard use. Check the other moving parts. These parts will be subjected to extreme thermal cycles (temperature swings). In a catalytic stove, is the combustor easy to remove so the required periodic cleaning and inspection can be done? Check the warranty. Does it include labor for the replacement of parts?

Quality and durability aren't necessarily synonymous. If you have purchased the former and treat it with care, you will get the latter.

The largest variable in stove emissions and hence in performance, is how the stove is operated by the user. You can have a code-approved installation and still have a hazardous amount of creosote in your chimney if you underfire (starve the fire of air) your stove. On the other hand, your stove and chimney could be badly sited, but if you operate the stove properly, you will still have little creosote in the stack. The key to safety is to burn hot fires and keep the chimney warm. This technique will not yield optimum fuel efficiency, but is the wisest compromise.

Do not think that a new stove will eliminate the need to monitor your fire? You will find when you read the owner's manual that even with the new stoves, there is as much involved in responsible woodburning as ever.

Aesthetics may dictate the stove design you choose. If the appliance will sit in the middle of your "parlor," it will be a prominent feature and perhaps even the focal point of that room. In this instance, let your taste play a major part in your choice.

The early cast iron parlor stoves were truly works of art. Nineteenth century wood and coal stoves represent a world more concerned with detail and balance, ornament and frivolity. The shape of the elaborate Franklins suggest medieval castles; the large parlor stoves invite a chilly soul to pull up a chair and put those icy boots up on their shiny plated "bumpers."

Certainly there is enough variety on the market to satisfy any taste.

Proper Sizing

To get the most efficient burn, the appliance's heat output must be matched to the space you intend to heat.

The typical house is composed of a number of spaces (rooms). The layout and connections between these spaces, and the overall R-value of the building envelope determine your stove's whole-house heating contribution. Generally, a wood stove can be expected to meet 80 percent of the heating requirements of its given space. During periods of extreme cold a thermostatically controlled heating system is appropriate as a supplemental back-up. During mild weather household heating requirements may be so low that the back-up system is again appropriate because it can cycle off, and thus save fuel that would otherwise burn incompletely or produce unwanted heat.

If you heat solely with wood, you may experience large temperature fluctuations or need to open windows frequently.

Factors in Sizing Your Stove

If you plan to heat one room, calculate the area in square feet (length x width). Heated air will enter the rooms above provided there is a floor register, stairway, or other means to create a circular loop of air. This air circulation pattern not only heats upstairs bedrooms, but is valuable for "dumping" excess heat that can build-up in the primary heated space. Excess heat usually occurs early or late in the heating season when there are large daily temperature swings. It can also happen in tight homes that have a large area of south-facing glass. Unless your floor plan is fairly "open," your stove will heat primarily the room it occupies.

In selecting a new wood stove, determine the right "size" (rated heat output) for your needs. A stove that is either too large or too small for the space to be heated will be inefficient, create more pollution, and may cause temperature discomfort. Follow the five steps below to get a rough idea of what sized stove to buy. For more information on wood stove selection and sizing, consult an expert (e.g., heating contractor, architect, or your local wood stove dealer).

1. On the following map (Figure 4-1), locate where you live and place an "X" at that point. Note where the "X" is in relation to the boundaries of the climate zones. For example, on the map an "X" has been placed at Little Rock, Arkansas, which is located in the middle of climate zone 5. The seven zones are determined by anticipated low temperatures ranging from below -20°F. to more than 30°F.
2. Determine the square footage of the area that you expect the wood stove to heat. Include the room the stove will be located in and perhaps the adjacent rooms. You will probably include only a portion of your house, unless you (1) have a small house, (2) are willing to live with big temperature differences within the house, or (3) have a means of distributing the heat to remote rooms.

Calculating Heat Requirements Based on Climate Zone

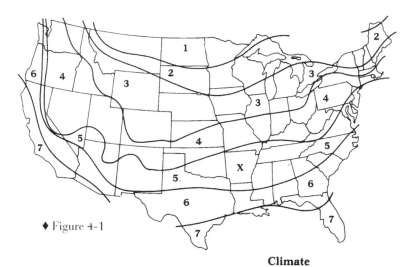

♦ Figure 4-1

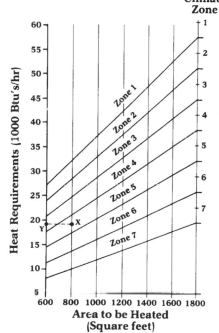

♦ Figure 4-2

Courtesy of *U.S. Environmental Protection Agency*

3. Look at the bottom line of numbers in Figure 4-2. Find the point that approximates the square footage estimate from Step 2. Next, draw a vertical line up from that point until you are in the right climate zone for your location. Look again at where you placed your "X" on the map. Place another "X" on the chart at a point that approximates your geographic position relative to the climate zone boundaries. (See the example calculation that follows.) From the "X" you made on the chart, draw a horizontal line to the heat requirement figures on the left side of the chart. This number is the unadjusted **maximum heat output** your new stove should be capable of producing.

4. Adjust your maximum heat output number by judging how "weatherized" your home is. If your home is a new, single-story wood house with 8-foot ceilings, double-glazed windows, and 3½ inches of insulation in the walls, 9 inches in the ceiling, and 6 inches in the attic knee walls (R-11, R-30, and R-19, respectively), no adjustment is necessary. However, if your house is drafty, has lots of windows, has high ceilings, or is poorly insulated, adjust the heat output value upward by 10 to 100 percent. The adjustment factor you choose should reflect how many and to what extent these factors are present. Similarly, if you have a very tight, well-insulated home with relatively few windows, reduce the heat output value by 10 to 50 percent.

5. Compare your adjusted heat output estimate with the heat output values on the labels of the EPA-certified stoves. Be sure that the high end of the heat output values is equal to or greater than the maximum heat output value you calculated in Step 4. In order to avoid buying too large a stove for your needs, also take into account your *average* heating needs, which will probably be one-half or less of the value you calculated in Step 4. Be sure that the low end of the range on the label is no higher than one-half the calculated heat requirement value. If you intend to use the stove during mild weather, ensure that the minimum heat output is about one-fourth the maximum value.

◆

Example: Choosing the Right Size Stove

A homeowner in Little Rock is considering a freestanding wood stove to heat his newly constructed, well-insulated 800-square-foot addition. He is trying to decide between two similar models. The larger unit says its heat output ranges from 12,000 to 50,000 Btus per hour; the heat output figures for the smaller one are 7,000 to 20,000 Btus per hour.

Using the map and chart on page 35, he first notes that Little Rock is in the center of zone 5. Next, on the chart he locates the point along the 800-square-foot vertical line that approximates the center of zone 5. This point is shown on the chart (Figure 4-2) by an "X." From here he draws a horizontal line to the left (marked by a "Y" on the chart). He has determined that for a typical house he would need about 19,000 Btus per hour for the coldest weather. His room addition, being unusually well-insulated and having relatively few windows, allows him to reduce the heat requirement somewhat. He estimates that a 20 percent adjustment is appropriate. He now calculates that the maximum heat output he will need is about 15,200 Btus per hour, with an average value of about 7,600 Btus per hour.

Having made this calculation, the homeowner can confidently purchase the smaller stove and still have sufficient heat. He also knows that had he bought the larger unit, he might have been uncomfortably warm most of the winter, paid too much money, operated the stove inefficiently, and created a safety hazard from creosote build-up.

How Heat Travels

Heat is delivered by **radiation**, **conduction**, or **convection**. Radiant energy exists in the form of wavelengths. It is not actually heat but energy that becomes heat when it is absorbed by surfaces. It is like the experience of standing in the bright sun on a cool morning and feeling heat from the sun being absorbed by the skin.

Conducted heat passes through a material. Different materials conduct heat at different speeds. Cast iron and steel, the materials out of which most stoves are made, conduct heat more quickly than insulation.

Convection is used in most home heating distribution and delivery systems. The heat-carrying medium is water or air.

Hot water or **hydronic** systems transport 160° to 180°F. water to finned tubing along the baseboards. Convection currents are created, causing warm air to circulate and heat the room.

In hot air systems, convection takes place at the furnace, and hot air either rises by gravity into the living spaces or is blown into them by a fan.

FREESTANDING WOOD STOVES

Although all stoves heat by radiation *and* convection, they are categorized as either circulating or radiant heaters. A circulating stove has an outer jacket on its vertical sides. As this jacket heats up, it radiates some heat into the room and reflects (re-radiates) some heat back to the stove. A convection current is established as the heated air rises between the body of the stove and the jacket, thus drawing more air in to continue the process.

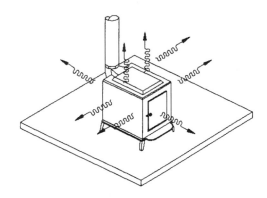

A radiant stove transfers its heat energy into the

♦ Figure 4-3. *Radiant woodstove.*

room in straight lines perpendicular to the radiating surface. In other words, radiant appliances heat what they "see." In older homes a radiant stove heats only the room it occupies. Registers and high speed fans can redistribute the heat from the heated objects in that room. And in well-insulated homes where the building envelope prevents heat transfer to the outdoors, a radiant stove will heat other parts of the house in proportion to their proximity to the stove. A radiant stove, ideally located in a two-story house, can heat the principal living areas

♦

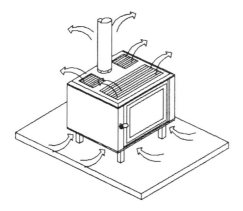

♦ Figure 4-4. *Convection woodstove.*

comfortably and keep bedrooms at a lower, comfortable temperature for sleeping.

The primary advantage of circulating or convection-type stoves is that their jackets moderate the "up-close" heat intensity and allow them to be installed with reduced clearances to combustibles (consult the manufacturer's listing on a plate affixed to the rear of the stove). If your installation must be near combustibles, check out a circulating or "close clearance" stove.

Antique Stoves

Most stoves built before World War II, and especially those built before the turn of the century, display a level of foundry precision not found in their modern counterparts. Not that the new stoves are not well made — they certainly are. They simply employ techniques or designs that don't require such precise castings. The older stoves were well suited to the homes and lifestyles of their owners. The uninsulated, drafty (by today's standards) homes were usually occupied during the day, so long burn times weren't essential. These stoves heat up more quickly than their modern counterparts, which is pleasant when you awaken after the temperature has dropped during a cold night. However, because air can leak in around the doors, lids, and draft openings, they burn more like fireplaces. The fires are difficult to control, require frequent stoking, and seldom achieve complete combustion. Nevertheless, antique stoves—potbellies and Franklins, parlor and box stoves — offer all the charm and beauty a proud stove owner could ever want.

Before firing up an antique stove, be sure you are burning the right fuel. Many of these stoves were designed to burn coal. These coal stoves have a grate for underfire air and a means for moving or "shaking" the grates free of clinkers and ash.

Be sure any antique or vintage stove you intend to use is structurally sound and has all its integral parts. If the stove has been unused for several years, a good cleaning and painting or polishing are in order. Lubricate the nuts and threads, and take the stove apart to clean the inside with a wire brush. Even better, buy a wire wheel for use with an electric drill for this purpose. This is dirty work, so do it outdoors and wear a mask.

Once you've removed as much rust and scale as you can, use a spray can to give the inside a couple of light coatings of high temperature stove paint. For wood stoves of cast iron, use Williams stove polish for the exterior. The polish gives a pewter-like finish and brings out the depth of the design. There are probably some shiny plated parts. If the plating is peeling or pitted, have it re-plated. It will be expensive, but the stove will look awesome. After you have reassembled the stove, fill any joints that let light through with stove or furnace cement.

From a design standpoint, cookstoves are a tribute to multiple uses. In addition to heating, baking and cooking, they provide warming ovens (places for rising bread or making yogurt) and storage for pot lids. Many had water jackets for heating water. Although the firebox on these stoves is small and the fire requires diligent refueling, combustion is vigorous and the iron mass provides excellent heat storage/transfer efficiency.

How do these stoves fit into the scheme of clean woodburning today? The antique and vintage stoves are appropriate for evening use and are capable of serious heating if there is someone around to feed them. They don't have the fuel efficiency of their modern counterparts but are unequaled for grace and charm.

Stovepipe Damper

When using an antique stove, install a damper in the stovepipe. For most of these stoves, you can't control the fire with the air intake as you can with modern "airtight" stoves. Also, start with some small

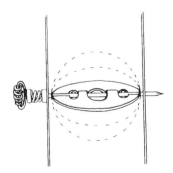

♦ Figure 4-5. *A stovepipe damper.*
Wood Heat Safety

fires before running it with a full load of wood. If the firebox is empty, lay a bed of ashes, sand, or castable refractory an inch thick to protect the floor from excessive heat. Make sure the door shuts securely.

AIRTIGHT STOVES OF THE 70S

The wood stove "boom" that occurred when OPEC raised the price of oil in 1973, was for many people an opportunity to heat with wood. We Americans had to relearn an old way of keeping warm. In fact, if this modern day experiment hadn't succeeded so well, wood stoves probably wouldn't be around today.

The people who started heating with wood 15 or 20 years ago are real pros now. They have evolved systems for every aspect of woodburning — from when to order firewood to making a safe ash dump. They know how much air to give the fire, when to clean the chimney, and how to revive a few coals. Their equipment has served them well.

Some of these stoves burn quite cleanly too. A few manufacturers of these stoves are still around and will admit to having made a number of design modifications along the way.

If you can't afford a new wood stove, be sure the secondhand stove is in good working order and can be safely installed in your space. However, the best place for some of the used stoves I've seen is the scrap metal bin. Ask your used stove seller why he is selling the stove. If you don't get a straightforward, sensible reply, keep your money in your pocket; you don't need an unwanted liability.

Airtight stoves feature a system of air inlets more sophisticated than those on antique stoves. Like antique stoves, airtights have a **primary air inlet** to let oxygen enter below the fuel to evaporate moisture trapped in the wood. In addition, there is a **secondary air inlet** to let air enter the stove above the coals to ignite the gases. As a result, the burns are longer and easier to control.

Many of these stoves also have **baffles** which force the gases into an "S" pattern before exiting the fire zone. By hampering the usual updraft, baffles maintain higher firebox temperatures. Higher temperatures result in more complete combustion, greater heat transfer, less creosote build-up, and more even heat.

After the EPA established performance and emission standards in 1985 for all new wood stoves, the airtights were re-designed and became high-tech, "low-emission" stoves. (See Chapter 5.)

FIREPLACE INSERTS

Fireplace inserts fit into the fireplace opening. They boost fireplace performance because the homeowner can control the amount of air which reaches the fuel wood. Some of these units feature blowers which further increase heat output.

Installation of an insert is quite simple but pay special attention to the venting system. The venting requirements for a fireplace and a wood stove are very different. Typically, fireplace flues are large enough to allow for the excess air that an open fireplace uses. In an improperly vented insert, the excess air and heat are quickly dissipated in an oversized chimney flue and the result is a sluggish draft. The fireplace chimney should be adapted by installing a continuous liner from the collar of the appliance to the top of the chimney.

Some early fireplace inserts (notably Better 'n Ben's) have an integral surround plate that closes off the fireplace opening. The plate supports the back end of the firebox, and prevents access to the outlet collar when the unit is in place. In these installations creosote forms inside the firebox, damper area, and smoke chamber as the smoke slowly finds its way to the flue. Cleaning is difficult, performance is reduced, and safety is compromised.

MASONRY HEATERS
Minimum Risk for Maximum Return

Early fire burners knew that a ring of rocks around the hearth would remain warm for several hours after the fire had gone out. They also knew the benefits of channeling air to the base of the fire through a tunnel dug in the earth. The early experiments with fire produced indigenous designs for iron-smelting, cooking and drying food, pottery firing, bathing, heating, and heat storage.

Russian stoves, Chinese k'angs, Korean ondols, Roman hypocausts, Swiss Kachelofens and Finnish contra-flows are all traditional forms of masonry heaters. Common throughout Europe, interest in these stoves was kindled in the United States in the 1970s.

Yankee magazine (February, 1978) carried an article about a "Russian Stove" being built by Basilio Lepuschenko, a cabinetmaker from Maine, and a "Finnish Fireplace" being built by a Maine dairy farmer, Sam Jakkola. The article triggered nationwide interest in masonry heaters. Jay Jarpe, a research engineer at the New Mexico Energy Institute, University of New Mexico, read the article. It prompted him to apply for and receive state funding to build and monitor eight test units in various parts of New Mexico. Workshops were organized in conjunction with his research and led to the popularity of Russian stoves on the West Coast.

In Finland government-sponsored research on design refinements to the Russian stove was undertaken at the Tampere University of Technology. Each year over 20,000 heaters and thousands of bakeoven and cookers are built; government-subsized mortgages specify the Finnish contra-flow heater as the primary heat source.

Albie Barden's keen interest in masonry heating took him to Europe and then to Finland where he worked with heater builder Heikki Hyytiainen. Their book *Finnish Fireplaces — Heart of the Home* inspired me to make a heater-bakeoven-heated-bench complex the focal point of our new home. It is highly recommended for anyone interested in this way of wood heating. Throughout the United States, Albie leads workshops on building the Finnish contra-flow heater. His enthusiasm and dedication are largely responsible for the increasing awareness of and interest in masonry heaters. David Lyle's sourcebook entitled *The Book of Masonry Stoves — Rediscovering an Old Way of Warming* is the definitive work on the subject and traces the rich history of masonry heaters throughout the Old World.

How Masonry Heaters Work

The principle of all masonry heaters in use today is the same: To burn a charge of wood as rapidly as possible with plenty of combustion air, for a short-lived but intense fire. The heat is captured in the masonry mass. The circulating gases pass through heat exchange channels and are exposed to a large surface area of masonry. The process is analogous to charging a battery. This gentle heat is then very evenly radiated into the living space over the next 12 to 24 hours.

Masonry heaters are not continuously fired like wood stoves. Instead, a fire of small diameter (no more than two to three inches) seasoned wood is laid in a criss-cross fashion or leaned vertically against the back wall to fill the entire firebox. A Finnish contra-flow heater will hold about 60 pounds of wood. The fire burns quickly and vigorously in an oxygen-rich environment, and flame temperatures in the firebox reach 1,600° to 2,000°F. Complete combustion is achieved within 5 to 10 minutes and proceeds for the remainder of the firing which can last from 45 minutes to 2 hours, depending on the size and moisture content of the wood and the firebox size.

The remaining coals are stirred and when the coals are no longer glowing, the air supply and/or damper is closed. This prevents the chimney from siphoning air through the heater and cooling the masonry mass prematurely. Gentle, even heat is radiated out from the mass until more heat is needed. One or two firings a day are usually sufficient: we have a third firing at night when temperatures consistently are below 10°F.

Heating Capability

Because of the large heating surface area and relatively low surface temperatures (maximum surface temperatures of 175°F are reached two to three hours after the firing), there is less air temperature stratification than with wood stoves. This low-level radiant energy provides for even heating without the convection currents of wood stoves which create warmer layers of air near the ceiling. Because there is so little air movement, there is less dust and therefore a healthier indoor environment. The result is a truly radiant heat system. Only the metal heater door gets hot enough to burn skin and then only when the fire is going. Our heater has a heated bench on the kitchen side. It is a true pleasure to come in from the cold and sit there with your back against the bricks and let the heat penetrate by gentle conduction.

To regulate a heating system without a thermostat is deceptively simple. As the surface temperature of the contents of a house go up, the same level of comfort is experienced with a lower air temperature, or to be more exact, the comfort zone of the house is greater over a wider range of air temperatures.

Safety

There is minimal risk with masonry heaters. Fred Schukal, a leading authority and innovator in the venting system industry, sums it up best; he calls the masonry heater a "fire in a safe."

◆

♦ Figure 4-6. *Masonry Heater.*   *Courtesy of Albert Barden III*
                                                    & Sandy Argifiotis

Efficiency

Masonry heaters are unsurpassed at converting firewood into radiant energy because their design and materials allow the fire to burn hot enough to release and consume the volatiles. Insulative or refractory firebrick is used in the combustion zones to minimize flame quenching. The rate of combustion is limited only by the moisture content and size of the fuel load. The extensive heat exchange channels in the masonry mass absorb and store heat from the exhaust gases for maximum heat transfer. Stack losses, or heat lost up the chimney, occur only during a firing, but high heat transfer is realized in the heated space for up to 32 hours after the fire is out and the damper is closed. Tests on the Finnish contra-flow heater at Tampere University showed overall operating efficiency in the 75 to 85 percent range — maximum return.

High operating efficiency is achieved by using correct burning techniques. Masonry cannot absorb an unlimited amount of heat energy. If more output is required, wait at least two hours before starting another fire; continuous firing stresses the masonry and is not recommended.

Because combustion air from the house is needed for only a few hours each day, the low humidity associated with metal stoves is eliminated. Since temperatures at the heater surface are below the boiling point of water, there is also a greater ratio of healthful negative ions in the air.

Until quite recently, the only way to install a masonry heater was to have it site-built by a mason like a traditional fireplace. Modular heater kits were first developed in Europe and recently have become available in this country. TuliKivi modular heaters and bakeovens utilize soapstone, the oldest material used in modular heater construction. Soapstone is the soft, dense, greyish material some early American sinks were made of. It is prized for its unsurpassed heat-retaining quality and workability and is now quarried for TuliKivi in Schuyler, Virginia by the New Alberene Stone Co., Inc. The heaters are of a Finnish contra-flow design. Royal Crown makes a traditional Swedish heater in stucco, stone, and tile. It incorporates a fan to provide additional quick heat transfer. Bio-Fire modular heaters from Austria are custom sized according to the space they will heat. They are available in a variety of tile facings or can be stuccoed. Norbert Senf's company, Masonry Stove Builders, located in Quebec, Canada, offers a modular Finnish contra-flow heater core named Heat-Kit. It incorporates locally purchased firebrick in the firebox and a secondary combustion chamber. **Firebrick** is a standard product and is used in site-built heaters for its ability to withstand the repeated thermal cycles. Also from Temp-Cast Masonry Heater Manufacturing Inc., Ontario, the Temp-Cast 2000 is a heater core of precast refractory units that are very quick and easy to assemble. Both the Heat-Kit and Temp-Cast cores are finished with a brick, stone, or stucco facing by a local mason.

This is only a partial list of modular masonry heaters in a young and expanding field. These modular heaters offer the benefits of a proven pre-engineered design. They save the time and skill involved in site cutting and laying up of firebrick. Options available in most masonry heaters include glass doors, built-in bakeovens, heated benches, and integral wood storage.

Masonry heaters are heavy. With the exception of the Bio-Fire, they require either a foundation or a reinforced concrete slab. They work best with an interior chimney which can be of a mass-insulated metal type.

Masonry heaters, like any heating system, work most efficiently in a well insulated space. They are the opposite of a quick response thin-walled metal stove, and therefore are inappropriate for a camp used only on weekends, for instance. Also, I wouldn't recommend one in a space with a lot of south-facing glass. Such spaces experience large daily temperature swings and like quick response heat. Masonry heaters will perform better if not placed on an outside wall. The Masonry Heater Association of North America, (see page 49 for complete address) can steer you to a qualified heater builder in your area.

Firing Up our Masonry Heater

My interest in masonry heating was "kindled" by reading an article on the virtues of Russian stoves while we were working on the plans for our new home.

Masonry heating didn't fit into our budget at first, but what finally "tipped the scale" for me was when an old customer who knew we were building asked me what kind of stove I was planning for our new home. I began telling him that masonry heaters were the ultimate way to heat with wood and went on to extol their virtues. Through that process I realized that I couldn't really be an advocate for something without firsthand experience.

Our masonry heater was built in April. By September we were anxious to fire it up. After building and lighting a small fire, I remembered I hadn't opened the air supply in the basement. By the time I got back upstairs, the smoke alarm was going off and smoke was pouring out around the doors. I had also forgotten to open the damper! Even then I had to make adjustments in the air supply to keep smoke from coming out around the bakeoven door. The interior heater dampness and cold made the draft sluggish. Now I pre-heat the flue with a couple of pieces of newspapers twisted and ignited in the clean-out. Every new routine requires some learning.

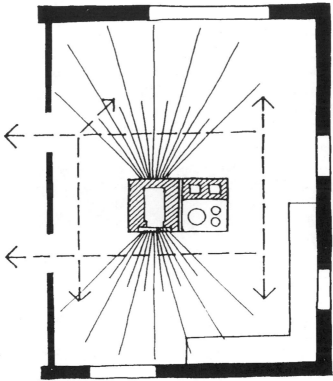

♦ Figure 4-7. *A masonry heater can be a complete radiant heating system, and should be integrated with the house design.*

Courtesy *Albert Barden & Heikki Hyytiainen*

We have the hang of it now, though. When you're not burning dry wood, the flames barely make it into the combustion chamber; with dry wood, the chamber is glowing yellow with flames. I'm determined to have next winter's wood split and seasoning before June. I'm hoping that with prime firewood we can have the evening fire closer to bedtime and the load will be burned and damper closed in 1½ hours instead of the 2 to 2½ hours it now takes. With improved combustion efficiency, we hope to cut our propane for the back-up heating system from 150 gallons to fewer than 100. Presently, with the thermostat set at 60°F., the circulator pumps hot water through our back-up system during the coldest early morning hours in the winter. That and about three cords of wood heated our 2,000 square foot saltbox in Plainfield, Massachusetts last winter (a climate of 7,500 heating degree days).

It is rewarding to have that much heating self-sufficiency without making woodcutting into a part-time job. I spend just enough time at it to make me appreciate my labor but not enough to feel it a burden.

We chose an optional bakeoven for its practicality. Any dinners that once went into the gas range oven — lasagna, chicken, casseroles — are all wood-fire baked.

For more information on masonry heaters, write to: Masonry Heater Association of North America, 11490 Commerce Park Drive, Reston, Virginia 22091.

CENTRAL HEATING WITH WOOD

If you prefer to keep your living space free of a hot, radiating body and the mess associated with firewood, there are a number of thermostatically controlled wood and multi-fuel furnaces that pro vide central heating. Whereas, a wood stove is both combustion chamber and heat exchanger, wood furnaces (as with conventional furnaces) separate these functions to some extent. Historically, wood furnaces have not produced a clean burn because: (1) to hold a large fuel charge, they had very large combustion chambers which made it difficult to provide a hot enough environment to combust the volatile gases, (2) the heat exchangers were located close enough to the combustion chamber to quench flames and therefore reduce the combustion of gases, and (3) some units responded to the thermostatic "off-cycle" by regulating the combustion process via the air supply. This contributed to smoldering fires and incomplete combustion.

Some units are "natural draft"; others employ a draft-inducing fan to assist in venting. Unfortunately, the units which require electricity to run the fan achieve relatively complete combustion and higher overall efficiencies. Some "induced draft" units are referred to as "gasifiers" because the gases are burned in a separate chamber. Since all woodburning devices burn volatile gases, this doesn't necessarily mean that they are clean burning or fuel efficient.

I am aware of at least one unit ("Tempest," by Dumont Industries) which operates like a masonry heater; the combustion chamber achieves high temperatures and complete combustion by intermittent firings. A large volume of water is heated by exiting gases and stored for circulation through the heat distribution system as needed. This particular design allows the combustion process to proceed regardless of the heating demand of the house, and can be fired occasionally during the summer to heat water for domestic use.

Domestic Hot Water

Domestic hot water is a significant benefit of a wood-fired heating system. A word of caution: Heating hot water under pressure is potentially dangerous. People have died as a result of explosions from superheated water creating pressures that could not be released by the system. Be sure your unit has been installed by a licensed heating contractor.

Multi-Fuel Furnaces

Multi-fuel furnaces fire one or more fuels in addition to wood. This allows the occupant to leave home for extended periods or switch to a back-up fuel when the woodpile's exhausted or she/he can't physically manage the firing.

Outside Boilers

These boilers live outdoors and either are self-contained or located in their own enclosure. Also known as Carolina Waterstoves, these units minimize the fire and health hazards associated with conventional wood heating systems.

PELLET STOVES

The pellet stove industry sprang up in the West as another answer to the 70s "energy crisis." They are an alternative to wood stoves in places where softwood forests predominate and/or firewood is in short supply. Pellet stoves are less like wood stoves than coal-burning stoves.

The fuel for pellet stoves is a refined product, like heating oil. It is easier to burn a standardized fuel cleanly when it is delivered at a consistent rate than it is to burn big pieces of wood in batches. In wood stoves heat output is regulated by the amount of air, not fuel, present in the stove. In pellet stoves the burn rate is controlled by the rate that the fuel enters the combustion chamber; therefore heat output is regulated by the amount of fuel burning. As you might imagine, combustion is quite clean when the fuel/air ratio is regulated this way.

Pellet stoves, along with masonry heaters, have achieved the lowest emissions of any EPA-tested appliances to date.

Pellet stoves require a fan to assist the combustion process and provide draft. If you live in an area where there are frequent power outages, ask about units that have a battery "back-up" system. Electricity to run the stoves costs between one and three cents an hour, depending on the stove and local rates.

> "To make pellets demands sophisticated equipment to achieve the proper temperature, pressure, and moisture. This process is similar to the way spaghetti or extruded metals are made. The pellet mill takes waste sawdust and chips and runs them through a dryer. This feedstock is then pulverized by a hammermill through a rotating die, where it is squeezed out and formed into pellets. Compressed at great pressure in the die, the pulp is formed into ¼-inch or ⁵⁄₁₆-inch diameter pellets ¼ – 1 inch long."
>
> from *The Pellet Primer* by Dan Melkon

Buying Pellets

Pellets are sold either in bags (40 pounds is the most common) or by the ton. A ton of pellets yields 13.5 MBtus of heat, and has the same heat value as a cord of spruce. Instead of taking up 128 cubic feet of space however, the pellets take up 48. The average price of pellets is currently $150 a ton in western Massachusetts. Were they available locally, you

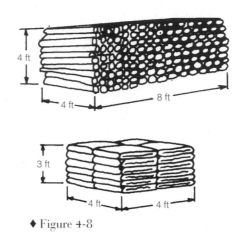

♦ Figure 4-8

would save the cost of shipping. As the demand for pellets increases, the price will fall.

Although wood is the predominant source of pellets, other biomass has potential as pellets, including nut shells, cotton by-products, grass stubble, and even garbage.

Freestanding stoves, fireplace inserts, furnaces, "add-ons," hot water heaters, and mobile home units are available for pellet burning. Some manufacturers offer a retrofit kit for converting a wood stove to a pellet burning heater.

The two primary designs to date are positive and negative pressure. The positive pressure design acts like a bellows on a sealed combustion chamber. The burned gases are pushed through the heat exchanger system and out the vent. The negative pressure stoves pull air into the unit through a draft-inducer fan located downstream of the burner.

The other major difference in pellet stoves is of how the fuel is fed into the fire. In **underfeed** units (see Figure 4-9) an auger turns and brings fuel into the "pot." **Overfeed** (see Figure 4-10) or

♦

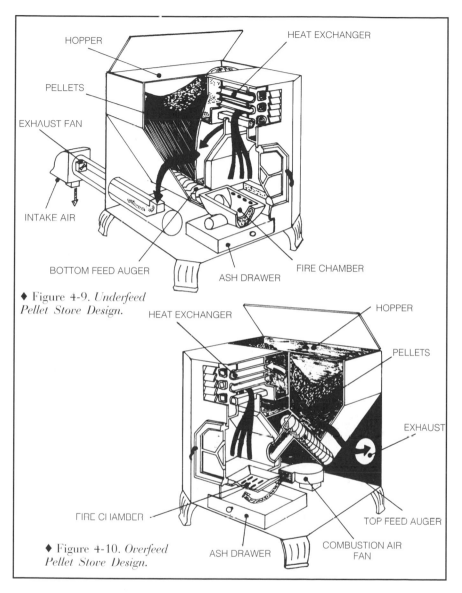

HOPPER

HEAT EXCHANGER

PELLETS

EXHAUST FAN

INTAKE AIR

BOTTOM FEED AUGER

ASH DRAWER

FIRE CHAMBER

♦ Figure 4-9. *Underfeed Pellet Stove Design.*

HEAT EXCHANGER

HOPPER

PELLETS

EXHAUST

FIRE CHAMBER

TOP FEED AUGER

♦ Figure 4-10. *Overfeed Pellet Stove Design.*

ASH DRAWER

COMBUSTION AIR FAN

"overfire" systems auger the fuel up an incline and drop it onto a grate or burn plate.

Athough pellet stoves can be vented directly to the outside with a proper vent kit, installers should run the connector up at least four feet before going out through the wall. This will provide the natural draft that will help combustion byproducts in the system vent in the event of a power outage. An adapted existing chimney is the preferred method of venting a pellet appliance.

♦

Actual operation usually consists of filling the hopper, lighting the fire, and setting the heat output control which can be a wall thermostat, or timer. Depending on hopper capacity and burn rate, refueling may be required every 12 to 48 hours, or more.

Maintenance, although minimal, is important. The moving parts require periodic lubrication, and the pot must be kept clean. Ash removal from the combustion chamber and vent is also important.

Under ordinary conditions, pellets produce no creosote. They are an existing technology that offers the romance and tradition of wood heat. Buy the unit from a reputable dealer. Having dealer support is especially helpful when you are unfamiliar with the product. Your satisfaction is important to them and the industry in developing this market. If your local wood stove dealer can't answer your questions about pellet stoves, write to: *Buying Guide to Pellet Stove*, Biomass Publications of America, PO Box 69333, Portland, OR 97201.

COAL BURNING STOVES

In some parts of the country, coal is the most abundant and cheapest fuel for home heating. Because of its sulfur content, coal emissions are blamed for the serious environmental threat of acid rain. Acidic precipitation which lowers ph levels, accounts for the death of lakes, the degradation of forest life, and the accelerated decay of virtually every man-made object that is exposed to the environment.

In his book *Heating with Coal* (Garden Way Publishing, 1980), John W. Bartok Jr. writes,

> *"A typical 800-megawatt electricity generating plant operating at an average of 75 percent capacity consumes 2.6 million tons of coal a year. It would take more than 500,000 homes in the northern climates consuming an average of five tons each to equal this consumption. It is true that power plants have scrubbers on the chimneys limiting the amount of pollutants exhausted, but still the pollution from 2.6 million tons of soft coal is significant. The coal commonly used in home heating has a sulfur content lower than the emission level from the power plant."*

◆

54

However, for lack of something better, we find ourselves relying on coal as a fuel to meet human needs. Coal has some endearing qualities, and there are many people burning coal who wouldn't trade fuels. Coal takes less space to store, and burns slower and hotter because of its higher density. Coal doesn't have to be cut, split or seasoned as does its arboreal counterpart.

Coal Formation

Coal is a combustible rock composed of vegetation, and formed over time with heat and pressure. The Coal Age was a period in the life of our planet when there was a uniform, moderate climate, and high levels of CO_2 — ideal conditions for vegetable growth. It is estimated that it took twenty feet of vegetable matter to form a one-foot layer of coal. Seams of coal are usually found in sloping beds separated by layers of clay and vary in thickness from a few inches to as much as several hundred feet. Beds may extend over hundreds of miles. Lignite, subbituminous, bituminous, subanthracite and anthracite are types of coal listed in order of their relative density.

Anthracite is the best type of coal for residential use. It is quite clean burning, has a high heat content, and generates little ash.

There are different sizes of coal. Depending on the area of the firebox and the size of the opening in the grate, every coalstove has a coal size best suited for it. The largest size is **stove** coal which is used in furnaces and heaters with a firebox larger than sixteen inches in diameter. The next size is **nut** coal which is best suited for residential stoves. **Pea** coal is used in kitchen ranges and smaller stoves. Because of its size, it packs tighter and requires a good draft in the chimney. It is also well suited to mild-weather burning.

Building a Coal Fire

The ignition temperature of coal is 200 to 400°F. higher than wood so it's more difficult to start a coal fire. Start with a small wood fire. Open the air supply on the ashpit door (primary air intake). Start with newspaper, kindling and some small pieces arranged loosely. Dry softwood is ideal. After a few minutes, add some larger pieces of wood. After this load is fully ignited, you can add a thin layer of coal over the top. Be patient: if you add coal too soon it will smother the fire and you will have to start all over again.

Once the first layer of coal is burning, add another thicker layer. Depending on the depth of the firebox, you may need to add a third load of coal. Once the stove is hot and beginning to heat the space, partially close the pipe damper and the primary air supply. This will keep the draft from exceeding the needs of the fire, yet sufficient to maintain combustion. The secondary air supply, located above the fire should also be left slightly open.

It's time to refuel once the load has burned down to half its original height. Open the pipe damper and air intakes before opening the loading door. This will increase draft and insure that gases go up the chimney when the door is open. Gently pull the coal bed toward the front and create a pocket for the new fuel. Again, be careful not to smother the fire.

Shaking the ashes

Most stoves have a mechanical means of moving or shaking the grate to allow ashes to fall into an ashpit. If there is no provision for shaking the grate, you will need to use a **fiddle stick** or **rod** to poke the ashes through. It's not necessary to shake the ashes when refueling, only when you sense that the fire is not getting enough air. A few short shakes should be all it takes before live coals start to drop through the grate. Overshaking wastes fuel and can disturb the load and even make the fire go out.

Overshaking or poking the fire can also form clinkers. A **clinker** is a very hot piece of coal that has been extinguished by the ash layer. It will not burn and cannot be shaken through the grate but must be removed before the next refueling.

Coal-burning Tips

1. Burn coal **only** in a coal-burning appliance. There are distinct differences between wood and coal burning stoves because the two fuels burn differently.

2. For new stoves, burn wood fires for the first week to break in the stove.

3. Do not use charcoal starter or any flammable liquids to start a coal fire. Charcoal is not recommended either because it gives off toxic fumes.

4. Since coal burns hotter and puts out steadier heat than wood, save it for the coldest months. Burn wood in the coal stove during spring and fall.

5. Clean the stove, connector pipe, and chimney in the off-season. Coal soot is acidic and corrosive. Use care when cleaning pipes. Wear leather gloves and a mask. Check for pin-hole leaks and replace any suspect parts. Clean and check the stove, especially the grates; replace any warped parts. A light coating of lubricant like WD-40 will inhibit rusting.

Chapter 5
A New Era: EPA-Certified Wood Stoves

With the increased production and use of residential wood-heating appliances and the detrimental effect these stoves had on air quality in densely populated woodburning regions, especially in river valleys and at high elevations, wood stoves soon became a target for regulation in Oregon and Colorado. Then, in 1985, the EPA established a performance standard for all new wood stoves. This became legislation as Section 111 of the Clean Air Act (CAA).

We now live in a new era of woodburning. John Crouch, emissions specialist for the Wood Heating Alliance, told me that wood stove development has moved forward more in the past five years than in the previous century. This is the result of EPA certification.

Most locales don't require that wood stove installations include an EPA-certified stove. The federal regulations apply only to the sale of new stoves; the used stoves are "grandfathered in." And some high quality airtight stoves are on the market at less than half the price of their new certified counterparts.

So why invest in a new clean-burning stove? Let's forget the decreased impact on the environment for the moment. After all, the lion's share of our environmental impact is the production of electricity and gasoline consumption. But I enjoy doing my part as a conscientious consumer. However if economics rule out a new stove for now, don't worry: they'll be around — and will only get more efficient.

Cost Analysis of Buying a New Stove

Before you decide you can't afford a new wood stove, do a simple cost analysis. Let's assume a new stove will require an additional $500 over the price of a used airtight stove in good condition.

Let's also assume that you would spend $100 a cord for four cords of wood in a heating season using that conventional airtight. If the efficiency of the new stove results in a 25 percent reduction in fuel use, you would save $100 (and some labor).

◆

If you pay back the $500 over two years, your payments with interest might total $600. At $100 per year fuel savings, the unit would have a six-year payback period or a 17 percent return on your investment. And we haven't accounted for the added life the new stove would have after it has paid for itself, as compared with the used stove. You might also save a couple of chimney cleanings during that period. All things considered, a more realistic return would be close to 30 percent, not counting the satisfaction derived from contributing to a healthier planet.

If you're reasonably sure you will be heating with wood in the years ahead, buying a new stove makes awfully good sense.

Wood Smoke versus Flue Gases

Open fires produce wood smoke — the colloquial term that refers to the visible, odorous gas that rises from the fire. However, the emissions from the new generation of wood stoves has been reduced significantly so that what was once called smoke is now called **flue gases**.

The EPA tests for the weight of particulates emitted at the rate of grams per hour. In addition to carbon monoxide, other products of incomplete combustion are POM (Polycyclic Organic Matter) and PAH (Polycyclic Aromatic Hydrocarbons) which include several toxic chemical compounds.

EPA Regulations

A wood heater as described by EPA regulations is a woodburning appliance used for space heating that meets all of the following criteria:

1. An air-to-fuel ratio averaging less than 35:1
2. A firebox volume of less than 20 cubic feet
3. A minimum burn rate of less than 5 kg/hour
4. A maximum weight of less than 800 kilograms (1760 lbs.).

The regulations explicitly exclude furnaces, boilers, cookstoves, and open fireplaces.

PM Standards

Wood heaters manufactured on or after July 1, 1988, or sold at retail on or after July 1, 1990, must meet certain PM (particulate matter) emissions standards (commonly referred to as **Phase I** standards); wood heaters manufactured on or after July 1, 1990, or sold at retail on or after July 1, 1992, must

Wood Heater Emission Limits (grams per hour)		
	Phase I (July 1, 1988- June 30, 1990)	Phase II (beginning July 1, 1990)
Catalytic	5.5	4.1
Noncatalytic	8.5	7.5

◆ Figure 5-1

EPA Federal Regulatory Commission

meet more stringent PM emission standards (**Phase II**). For each phase there are separate emission limits for catalytic wood heaters and for non-catalytic wood heaters as specified in Figure 5-1.

Many of the stoves that met the first phase of the EPA's certification program were modifications of existing stove designs. To meet Phase II certification, the requirements were so stringent that most manufacturers had to "start from scratch." Not only did the stove have to meet Phase II emissions in laboratory tests, but also in the field.

Stove testing is done with well-split, dry firewood. A typical stick is pie-shaped with numerous radial cracks and contains no more than 20 percent moisture by weight. (This may sound like a lot, but it is actually less than one half the moisture content of "green" wood.) Ideal size depends on the stove but the range is from three to six inches measured across the greatest distance.

To meet the Phase II standards, it was necessary to design a stove that was less sensitive to variable conditions such as venting systems and even owner operation. Low emissions for a burn cycle had to be achieved without close attention paid to fuel load configuration or even air supply after the initial 15-minute high rate of burn.

To operate your new wood stove correctly: Read and follow the owner's manual. Each stove operates a little differently. After you've read the manual, keep it handy. You will probably need to refer to it once or twice before you have mastered your stove.

EPA-CERTIFIED STOVE DESIGNS

To achieve clean combustion and prevent air pollution, the new EPA-certified stoves are designed using one of two technologies: catalytic combustors or high-tech, non-catalytic stoves (modified airtights which burn more efficiently).

High-Tech Non-Catalytic Stoves

High-tech, non-catalytic stoves are designed to increase efficiency and decrease emissions. This has been accomplished by decreasing firebox size, increasing turbulence by sophisticated oxygen delivery patterns, and adding baffles to insure that the smoke is burned in the combustion chamber. Many of the fireboxes are also lined with firebrick to create hotter fires.

Non-catalytic stoves perform as well as they do because of ingenious firebox design. They provide even heat, and because there is no catalyst to decay, maintenance costs are lower.

Catalytic Stoves

Catalytic stoves are fitted with a ceramic honey-combed combustor coated with a noble metal (usually platinum or palladium). This catalyst reacts chemically at a given temperature without being appreciably changed during the reaction. Smoke consisting of volatile gases is directed through the combustor which acts as an afterburner. The combustor reduces the ignition temperature of the volatile gases, allowing them to burn at roughly half their normal temperature. Ordinarily combustible gases burn at 1,000°F.; in a catalytic stove the smoke burns at 600°F.

There are important design considerations for a successful catalytic stove. The placement of the combustor is critical; the combustor must be in a high heat area of the firebox but protected from contact with actual flames which would destroy the unit.

Secondary air inlets and baffling are employed to provide oxygen and turbulence in the combustor area which are essential for complete combustion.

For the stove and combustor to reach steady state temperature, a **bypass damper** allows smoke to exit the stove directly during start-up. After exhaust temperatures of 600°F. for 15 minutes (or whatever the manufacturer specifies), the combustor is engaged.

Phase II catalytic stoves are user friendly in the sense that they can be loaded full of fuel and after combustor "light-off," they burn at a low rate for the rest of the cycle. This is exactly how many airtight stoves were operated and why woodburning was targeted as a source of air pollution. However, this mode of operation is a must for people who are absent during the day, but who want to return to a warm house at night. In addition, catalytic stoves achieve overnight clean burns.

The *advantages* of catalytic stoves are many. They are able to heat a larger space or heat the same space for a longer period of time than their non-catalytic counterparts. The firebox of a catalytic unit is larger than the optimum size for complete combustion because it "cleans up" the burn before the gases leave the firebox. If you want to heat a moderately sized, energy efficient house with wood and consistently long burn cycles, you might choose a catalytic stove.

The *disadvantages* of catalytic stoves is also their strength — the combustor itself. In order to function properly, the combustor must seal off the rest of the smoke path and remain free of ash build-up. For proper operation, it is absolutely essential to inspect the combustor on a regular basis and to clean it when necessary.

If you are not willing to do this maintenance yourself, you will have a maintenance expense. The combustor degrades over its normal lifetime or roughly five years. Replacement costs are $100 to $150.

A catalytic stove is more draft sensitive. Because the combustor restricts flow, a minimum -.03 draft is required. (See Appendix B for other possible problems.)

Catalytic Stoves versus Non-Catalytic Stoves

Having cleaned chimneys that have vented both types of stoves, I have found that generally the non-catalytic chimneys are cleaner. I attribute this to the catalytic stove operator who either relies on the combustor to compensate for wet wood or doesn't wait for the unit to reach the critical "light-off" temperature — usually 600°F. for 15 minutes. (See Appendix A for a summary of field studies on emissions for various wood stoves.)

New Stove Amenities

Virtually all of the new stoves have fire-viewing glass. Watching a fire is half the enjoyment to me. The glass allows you to see what your fire is doing — if it needs more wood or more air. Many earlier stoves offered high temperature glass as an option, but the glass never stayed clean.

Another feature that has been adopted by stove manufacturers is an ash drawer. It allows you to empty the ashes without letting the fire die out.

CHAPTER 6

Chimneys and Wood Stoves: An Intimate Relationship

There are four factors that contribute to efficient, environmentally responsible woodburning: the appliance, the fuel, the user, and the chimney. The user's habits can be modified; wood size and dryness can also be adjusted. But the chimney is permanent, and if it already exists, it may determine your choice of stove. On the other hand, you may opt for a factory-built metal stack.

Remember the chimney is an integral part of the heating system. It doesn't just vent gases. It affects the combustion process. It must withstand the forces of time, temperature, and weather. The safety of any chimney is greatly enhanced by preventing the accumulation of flammable creosote.

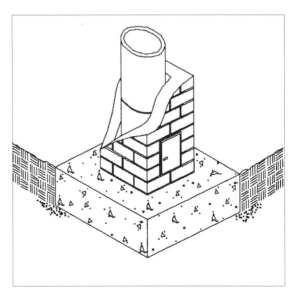

◆ Figure 6-1

Modern solid fuel appliances are designed for maximum performance in chimneys that provide sufficient draft. This requires a venting system that meets specific requirements for cross-sectional area and can maintain minimum flue gas temperatures.

TYPES OF CHIMNEYS

NFPA 211 codebook defines the minimum requirements for two accepted types of chimneys: masonry and metal.

Masonry or Site-Built Chimneys

A modern masonry chimney is built by a mason out of brick or "block." It is constructed with an outer casing of brick, concrete, or stone, and an inner clay (a.k.a. terra cotta) flue liner. The outer casing supports the liner and provides a heat buffer between liner and building. The liner is laid up inside the casing with a dead air space between so that heat will not be conducted to the outer casing and so that the liner can expand and contract. Heat transfer from the liner to the casing is undesirable; it decreases flue gas temperatures.

Current NFPA codes require that masonry chimneys be lined with a fire clay flue lining or the equivalent. Most chimneys built after 1930 have liners, but before the days of clay flue tiles, masonry chimneys were built with only a single layer of brick. To discover whether your chimney is lined, go up on the roof. The flue liner should extend beyond the block or brick walls. If your chimney is unlined, don't use it. Unlined masonry chimneys, if they are in good condition, must be retrofit

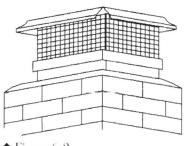

◆ Figure 6-2

with a stainless steel, cementious, or refractory lining system before they can be used to vent a wood stove.

While you're on the roof, shine a flashlight down the stack. Better yet, if the sun is out, use a mirror to direct sunlight into the flue. The liner should be smooth to promote good air flow, gas-tight so that maximum draft can be achieved, and as straight as possible. The chimney should terminate with a rain cap and spark screen. A clean-out at the base is convenient for soot and creosote removal, and for periodic inspection.

Clay Tile Liners

Clay tile liners are the most economical lining material and when properly built, provide a smooth, tight smoke path. They also decrease heat transmission to nearby combustibles during a chimney fire, decrease drafts between adjoining flues, protect the masonry from creosote deterioration, and because they do not respond as quickly to sudden changes in temperature (as the masonry does), they help contain chimney fires.

In most cases, a properly built masonry chimney with modular 8x12 rectangular tile liners is adequate for venting the new generation of solid fuel appliances with a 6-inch collar. An 8x8 liner would be better.

Testing, however, has found that clay tiles fail when subjected to the thermal shock (sometimes in excess of 2,100°F.) of a chimney fire. The sudden extreme temperature rise causes square and rectangular tiles to expand at different rates and the brittle nature of the material can result in **stress relief cracking**. Once this happens, flue gases are no longer contained and the potential for a house fire is greater. In addition, tile-lined chimneys are more likely to accumulate creosote—another fire hazard—than are stainless, cementitious, or refractory lined chimneys.

Round Flues

For exiting gases, a round flue is better than a square or rectangular flue. Not only does it provide the maximum volume with the least surface area within a given length, but it matches the shape of the rising, swirling gases. However, square and rectangular liners are much more prevalent. Perhaps tile makers knew it was more difficult to cut the mitre joint necessary to join tile sections at angles with round tiles than with square or rectangular ones. But round clay flues are available. Some even have a lap joint which takes the guess work out of centering, and ensures a tight seal. The "tee" connection is also difficult to site cut, although I have seen round tee sections at the local masonry supply yard.

A round flue will withstand the damage that can occur from the thermal shock of a chimney fire better than other shapes.

Refractory and Pumice-based Liners

These pre-cast flue sections are very heat resistant and have great potential in new construction. They come in round, square, and rectangular dimensions.

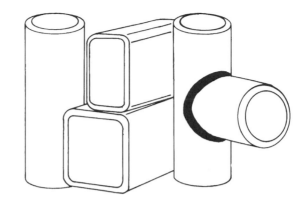

◆ Figure 6-3. *Different shapes of flue liners.*

Lining an Existing Masonry Chimney

An existing unlined masonry chimney can be retrofit with a cast-in-place or metal liner.

Metal Liners

To repair or upgrade your chimney by installing a metal liner, consult a chimney professional. Don't try to do chimney relining yourself. It is a technical procedure, requires special tools, and can be dangerous. UL-listed relining systems aren't available from retailers because manufacturers won't warrant their products unless they are professionally installed.

Stainless steel liners are available in rigid sections and in continuous flexible conduits. The rigid sections are less expensive but can only be retrofit in chimneys without bends. Because stainless steel expands with heat, room for expansion should be left. Stainless liners expand lengthwise as well. Therefore there should be provisions at the termination for them to slide up and down. Flexible liners are available in oval and rectangular shapes for tight flues. They can be pulled up from the chimney top or dropped down from above, as well as pulled through non-straight flues. There are many alloys of stainless steel. The 300 series (austinetic) stainless should be used for solid fuel stacks. Liners that are contained in exposed cold portions of the chimney should be insulated with appropriate materials. Some lining systems have passed UL testing with chimneys that are touching combustibles.

Cast-in-Place

A number of companies sell "poured liner" systems. This process was developed in Europe and enjoys a long history of success. It involves pouring a cementious mixture into the chimney either around an inflated bladder or onto an inverted cone that is pulled up through the mix as it is poured in. The mixture is insulative and resistant to creosote fire damage, and can be used to strengthen old chimneys.

OPEN FIREPLACE CONVERSIONS:
Hearth Stoves and Inserts

Fireplace Conversion

An open fireplace can be converted for venting a woodstove or fireplace insert. These installations should be done by a trained installer. They require venting the appliance directly to the flue and preferably directly to the outside using one of the relining systems discussed earlier in the chapter.

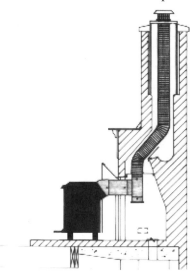
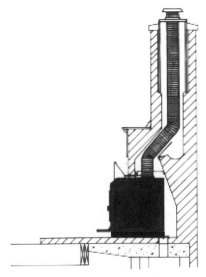

◆ Figure 6-4. *Hearth Stove.*   ◆ Figure 6-5. *Fireplace Insert.*

◆

If your woodstove is going to be vented using the fireplace, it is often referred to as a **hearthstove** (see figure 6-4). You can also install a stove designed for use only in a fireplace — an **insert** (see figure 6-5). This is a stove that rests on the floor of the firebox and uses a surround plate that closes off the rest of the fireplace opening so you don't see the connector pipe. The plate makes the installation look finished and attractive.

If you are going to vent a freestanding woodstove through the fireplace, you will have to maintain required clearances from wood mantles and trim and extend the hearth out to protect combustable floors. Avoid venting a large, top-venting stove straight up through the damper. Remember, this is an adapted use of the fireplace. If the stove top lies just under the lintel (the angle iron that supports the masonry spanning the top of the fireplace opening), it would conduct more heat to wood framing in the wall above than an unaltered fireplace would — perhaps enough for pyrolysis to occur. (See Chapter 8 p. 89.)

Direct Connects

For any fireplace conversion, a "direct connection" to the first flue tile is now required. This connection keeps the gases from entering the large, dome-shaped smoke chamber where they will cool before entering the flue itself. However, this makes chimney cleaning more difficult. Not only does the appliance have to be moved out of the way, but also the connector assembly must be removed so access can be gained to the smoke shelf; creosote frequently falls on the smoke shelf during flue cleaning. On exterior chimneys this problem can be solved by installing on the outside of the chimney an access door which opens into the smoke chamber just above the smoke shelf.

The "direct connection" is only a partial solution to the problem of heavy creosote build-up. And the need to re-install the appliance after every cleaning makes maintenance impractical. I recommend the installation of a stainless steel lining system for any hearth stove or insert installed in a fireplace with a flue cross-sectional area greater than twice the cross-sectional area of the appliance outlet collar. NFPA 211 8-5.5 (b) calls for the cross-sectional area of the flue to be "no more than three times the cross-sectional area of the flue collar of the appliance."

An appliance with an 8-inch flue collar can be installed in a 12" x 12" tile-lined masonry chimney provided there is a direct connection from the appliance collar to the first flue tile, and the stove is operated in the "door open" mode. However, in the closed-door mode there usually isn't sufficient flue-gas heat to compensate for the extra flue collar area. In this instance the stove will burn more efficiently if the flue is relined with 8-inch diameter pipe.

The efficiency of an oversized flue is analogous to placing a kettle of water six inches above your kitchen range, turning the heat all the way up, and expecting the water to boil. That's how an oversized masonry chimney flue impacts stove performance. It's an engine on the verge of stalling.

Pre-fabricated Masonry Chimneys

There are three companies that presently offer a pre-fabricated, masonry chimney system. **Isokern U.S., Inc.**, offers a liner and outer casing chimney system and modular masonry fireplace. These components use a volcanic pumice as the aggregate in the cementious mix to produce a material which insulates, reflects heat, and is more stable under thermal stress. **Chimtek Inc.**, manufactures an inner chimney liner of volcanic pumice aggregates and refractory cements. A secondary liner made of leca (a high grade expanded clay aggregate) is the insulating infill between the inner liner and a masonry (brick, block, or stone) outer casing. **National Supaflu Systems, Inc.**, offers both a modular block chimney system called Supa-Block, and a liner-infill system.

These systems have been tested to a rigorous safety standard, UL 1777, which exposes them to the high temperatures achieved during chimney fires. In addition, they are truly high-performance chimneys; they maintain critical flue gas temperatures even when venting the high-efficiency heating appliances that exhaust flue gases at a lower temperature. These insulated, reflective flues maintain draft and therefore reduce the risk of back venting. They also reduce the risk of moisture condensation on the inside of the flue, and the formation of sulfuric acid (most common in coal and oil flues) and hydrochloric acid which can occur in the natural and L.P. gas venting systems.

Another advantage of Supaflu's Supa-Block chimney and Isokern's chimney is that the chimney (a warranted product) can be erected in the same time and with the same skills as a block and tile chimney.

Another option in new chimney construction is to build the exterior casing of the chimney and install a chimney liner.

Check with the local building inspector or fire chief to ensure that you have their approval for what you are doing.

METAL STACKS

Thermosiphoning Chimneys

Some early metal chimneys were of a triple-wall thermo-siphoning design. Triple wall pipe is three pipes of graduated sizes which nest within one another. Cold air is drawn down between the outer two surfaces, rises between the next two — hot air rises — while smoke and gases exit through the innermost pipe. The theory was that, in the event of a chimney fire, air circulation would increase, thereby protecting combustibles from exposure to the heat. But they worked this way under normal operation as well. This prevented the inner wall — the flue itself — from creating a good draft. More important, creosote tended to collect on the inner wall.

Factory-Built, Pre-Fabricated Metal Chimneys

Factory-built metal chimneys require less heat to maintain high flue gas temperatures and are, therefore, less prone to condensation and creosote formation.

Metal chimneys can withstand a chimney fire but should be closely inspected for any distortion or discoloration. If these signs are seen, the chimney should be replaced.

Factory-built or pre-fab metal chimney systems are easy to retrofit into existing buildings, don't require masonry skills, and, when installed according to the manufacturer's instructions, meet the minimum safety standard set by UL 1777. Metal chimneys for wood stove venting should be "all-fuel, Class A" and insulated. They should carry a UL-approved listing, or certification by a recognized independent testing lab that the product has been tested to UL standards.

Some metal chimneys are "packed" with loose fill insulation. This insulation can settle, leaving the top of each chimney section without insulation and the protection it provides. Another problem with "pack" metal chimneys is that the sections exposed to weather can eventually lose water tightness. If insulation becomes wet, the sections should be replaced. Suspect sections will show excessive creosote build-up and, once removed, will weigh noticeably more. Some metal chimneys incorporate a blanket type of insulation and an air space which would offer better performance over time.

Metal stacks are expensive but are much easier to retrofit than masonry chimneys. They can also start at the ceiling of the room the stove is in, whereas a masonry chimney must start from a footing below the frost line or on a basement floor.

If the metal chimney passes through living space, it must be framed in and enclosed in a "chase." This will take up a "column" of space about 20 inches square.

CHIMNEY PLACEMENT

Traditional early American Capes, saltboxes and Colonials all had central masonry chimneys. There are good reasons why, especially in northern climates.

Exterior Masonry Chimneys

Here in New England, masonry chimneys located outside the building pose a specific challenge for wood stove venting. Because outdoor temperatures are so cold, it is difficult to keep escaping flue gases above the dew point. On many mid-winter nights when an overnight burn is under way, flue walls wick away heat faster than the rising gases can replace it. The result is condensation of water vapor and other combustion by-products.

Chimneys located on an exterior wall are "slow starting": they contain a column of cold air in winter that is waiting to enter the living space when you open the damper. This means a greater likelihood of a smoking fireplace or wood stove.

Interior Masonry Chimneys

An interior chimney is preferable to an exterior one. It requires less maintenance, and deterioration from weather is significantly reduced. Also the chimney air is at ambient temperatures which creates an initial updraft when the damper is opened.

An interior masonry chimney is a valuable **heat sink**. When the chimney is in use, the hot gases going up the flue impart some heat to the masonry. Also, the masonry is capable of holding and storing the ambient heat in the building, whatever its heat source.

Is an interior chimney still energy efficient given the fact that it must penetrate the roof? Although the chimney acts as a **thermal bridge**, wicking away its heat to the outside as it leaves the building, the heat loss isn't significant.

Chimney Crown

The critical part of any chimney is the sloping crown above the roof which sheds water away from the exposed flues. It should be of concrete, preferably re-enforced, and be at least two inches thick. When the crown is cast, there should be an expansion joint around the flues so that they can expand as they heat up. Seal the joint with silicone. Often this crown develops cracks which let the water in. The structure then begins to deteriorate from freeze-thaw cycles. Porous brick can **spall.** This is a deterioration where water penetrates the brick facing, causing it to break off. A chimney waterproofing treatment is the solution in this case.

An Energy Efficient Chimney

If energy efficiency is a priority, try the following construction which I chose for my house. The outer brick structure and flues stop in the attic a couple feet below the roof. I attached insulated metal chimney sections to the last round clay flue tiles. The flue tiles made a "tongue" which fit into the "groove" of the bottom end of the metal chimney sections. Use "RTV" silicone (rated to 900° F.) to make an airtight seal.

The joint is just below a wire lath-and-stucco "crown" that seals off the airspace around the flues at the end of the brick chimney.

I then plumbed down and cut the roof penetration large enough so that the metal chimney could exit through a 2x4-framed plywood chase with adequate clearances to

(continued on next page)

---

combustibles. The chase is oversized to reach just over the roof ridge. This eliminated the job of cricket construction and flashing the standing-seam metal roof.

The chimney chase was near square and massive looking. Galvanized metal lath was screwed onto the plywood and stretched over a temporary frame. I used two layers of lath over this frame to form a half-round rain cover, and two layers over an angle-iron-braced frame that formed the sloping chimney crown itself.

Don't break the lath at a corner or the stucco will crack there. If you choose to insulate at the roofline rather than insulating the chase itself, provide some weathertight ventilation for the chase or you will have condensation problems.

The rain cap was stuccoed first from the outside and the plastic-covered temporary form removed so that the crown could be built and stuccoed with the rest of the structure including the underside of the rain cap. The entire structure was then stuccoed twice, one scratch coat and a smooth, finish coat in white.

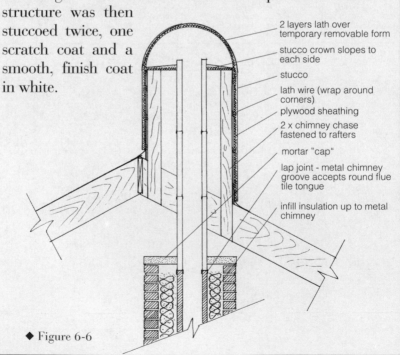

2 layers lath over temporary removable form

stucco crown slopes to each side

stucco

lath wire (wrap around corners)

plywood sheathing

2 x chimney chase fastened to rafters

mortar "cap"

lap joint - metal chimney groove accepts round flue tile tongue

infill insulation up to metal chimney

◆ Figure 6-6

Illustration by Harold Westwood

Exterior Metal Chimneys

Metal chimneys make more sense located within the building for the same reasons masonry chimneys do; metal chimneys attached to the exterior of a house perform poorly.

DRAFT

I recently heard a wood stove manufacturer refer to the chimney as "the engine that drives the wood stove." Any vertical column of air whose temperature is higher than the air surrounding the column will cause that column of air to rise. Warm air is lighter than cool air because the molecules vibrate more and expand or become less dense. This is how hot air balloons, gravity heating systems, and circulating stoves work. In chimneys this phenomenon is called **draft**. Maintaining a good draft is essential for optimum stove performance.

Draft is measured in hundredths of inches of a column of water. A typical draft reading is $-.03$ to $-.10$ column inches of water. (Corning specifies that their catalytic combustors not be used unless the chimney draft range is between $-.03$ and $-.06$.) A good draft allows you to start a fire easily and to reload the stove without permitting smoke to escape into the room. A good draft also helps a fire to burn, rather than to smolder, when the air supply is reduced.

The draft (suction or negative pressure) in the chimney brings the air into the stove and creates the turbulence that mixes air with the fuel gases. If the stove is designed so that this mixture is exposed to temperatures sufficiently high to allow the mixture to burn, clean combustion will result.

Efficiency and emission ratings for new appliances are calculated from laboratory installations which use a test chimney that is vertical, insulated, 18-feet high, and fitted with a flue collar of the same dimension as that of the appliance. Under these conditions, an insulated metal chimney achieves better performance statistics than the typical masonry chimney. The insulated metal pipe has less mass than a masonry chimney and therefore requires less heat to reach temperatures near those of the flue gases. Maintaining high flue wall temperatures is the key to maintaining a good natural draft, which in turn is the key to achieving high performance figures for a given wood stove.

◆

Draft in a Masonry Flue

The typical masonry chimney has either an 8x18 or an 8x12 flue opening. However, fireplace flues may be as large as 12x12, 12x16, 16x16, or 24x24. An 8x8 tile liner with a 7x7 inside dimension and a cross sectional area of 49 square inches is 73 percent larger than the 28.27 square inches required for an appliance with a 6-inch stove collar. The larger the cross sectional area of the flue, the more Btus are required to heat up the flue walls. As mentioned earlier, warm flue walls don't rob heat needed for high flue gas temperatures which are essential for a good draft and for the associated turbulence needed for clean combustion. A typical masonry single flue chimney takes about ten times more Btus per foot to heat up than a comparable mass-insulated metal chimney.

How Does Flue Size Affect Safety?

Unless wood combustion in the stove is complete, unburned volatiles go up the chimney. If the flue walls are above the dew point of the gases, the gases escape into the atmosphere, and creosote formation in the chimney is minimal. If the flue walls are below the dew point of the gases, the vapor condenses on the walls as flammable **creosote**. In cases of cooler flue walls and more incomplete combustion (denser smoke), this build-up can form a shiny, or even sticky, baked-on glaze. This is the most potentially dangerous situation because the creosote is difficult to remove and may even penetrate the flue tiles themselves.

The best precaution is prevention. If the size of your stove is the primary culprit (too large and powerful for the space), do one or more of the following:

- Leave windows open to vent excess heat. This allows you to burn with more combustion air, which means more heat will be available to travel up the chimney.
- Leave internal dampers or baffles in the open position. (This may compromise overall efficiency by reducing heat transfer efficiency.) This measure is not necessary once the fire is at the "burning coals" stage.
- Burning larger pieces of wood will allow you to burn with more air which will keep the chimney warmer.

- Replace your stove with a properly sized, clean-burning model. This is the best option for reducing the risk of fire in the chimney and, if necessary, line or reline the chimney to match the size of the stove collar.

Draft Problems

The strength of the updraft in a chimney is related to the temperature differential between the flue interior and the outside ambient air. Burning a hotter fire can overcome the lack of natural draft. The early airtight stoves were often too large for the space they were heating. What appeared to be a sluggish draft was really caused by underfiring the stove. The smoldering fire didn't provide enough heat in the flue to sustain a draft. If your appliance is properly sized for the space you are heating, check the following solutions for a weak or sluggish draft.

1. *Lack of combustion or "make-up" air.*
   Lack of combustion or *flow reversal* air is usually associated with fireplaces. Not only does an open fire consume a lot of air in the combustion process, but excess air must be available to maintain the draft. If the fireplace was properly built, cracking open a nearby window is the solution. If the wind is blowing, open a window on the windward side

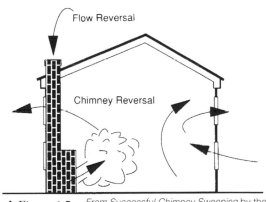

Flow Reversal

Chimney Reversal

◆ **Figure 6-7**   *From Successful Chimney Sweeping* by the Chimney Safety Institute of America.

of the house. Wood stoves, on the other hand, require relatively little air. For this reason, proper draft is a more delicate balance in the steady operation of the system. Sometimes it is necessary to establish a draft in a "cold" chimney. Light a twisted newspaper near the flue collar, or at the damper of a fireplace to start a draft. You may need to repeat this several times.

Insufficient combustion air is more common in today's energy efficient "tight" houses. With decreased air infiltra-

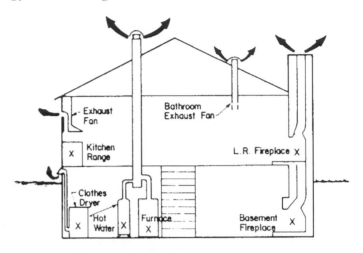

◆ Figure 6-8. *Venting appliances rely on air infiltration for intake air supply to provide "make-up" air.*

Fireplace Technology in an Energy Efficient World, by H. Morstead.
Courtesy Sleepy Hollow Chimney Supply, LTD.

tion, appliances which vent to the outside tend to depressurize the building. This may cause the chimney to become the source of make-up air — a dangerous situation. The solution is to: 1) open a window, 2) ensure a slight positive pressure with a fan (placed at ground level), or 3) install a glass door enclosure.

2. *Lack of chimney height.*
    Many chimneys do not meet the NFPA code requirements for height. If a lack of combustion air is not the problem, and running the stove a little hotter isn't comfortable, you can extend the height of the chimney, install an insulated stainless liner to decrease the flue size, or run the stove at a higher temperature and use a fan to distribute the warm air.

3. *Excess volume.*
    To sustain a good draft in an oversized flue, requires more heat than is available from the exhaust output of the appliance. The result can be heavy creosote build-up of the

———◆———

hard-to-clean, tar-like form. If the flue is larger than the flue collar and you are not able to sustain a good draft, burn a little more wood at a faster burn rate to create a warmer flue. Or reline the chimney.

4. *Undersized chimney.*
In this reverse situation, the problems worsen significantly. When a chimney is smaller than the smoke outlet of the stove or too small for the fireplace opening, the amount of smoke leaving the stove is too great for the chimney to handle. The symptomatic smoke-in-the-house can lead to early identification of the problem.

In the case of a fireplace, reduce the size of the fireplace opening or reconfigure the firebox and weir. The simplest solution is to install a smoke guard across the top of the opening (straight lintels only). This remedy helps any fireplace that tends to smoke, whatever the reason.

5. *Mild weather, bends, offsets, and high altitude.*
These factors must be taken into account. Any of them may produce continued smoking in a fireplace; a draft inducer fan can be installed at the top of the chimney to provide the necessary draft.

6. *Draft dilution.*
Any opening into the flue other than the appliance vent hole will try to equalize any pressure difference and dilute the draft. An open clean-out door, for example, will dilute the draft. A second flue in the same chimney if it isn't totally isolated, will dilute the draft in the first flue. If the two flues are connected at the base of the chimney, a wad of fiberglass insulation stuffed in through the clean-out door will separate the two flues. A poorly built or damaged flue can admit outside air. Do a smoke test to check for leaks. If the smoke comes out the exterior of the chimney, there is no longer containment and the chimney should be relined.

7. *Obstructions.*
Bird and squirrel nests and raccoons can be kept out of the stack with a chimney cap that has mesh sides. Excess mortar can also obstruct the draft. If it protrudes into the flue, the mortar can usually be chipped off.

———◆———

Draft-Inducing Fans

One way to cure a smoking fireplace is to install a draft inducing fan that mounts on the top of the chimney a few inches above the flue. The motor is powered by a switch that would be installed near the fireplace. This is recommended when smoking is due to uncorrectable site or construction factors and alterations to the fireplace (smokeguard, glass enclosure, etc.) are ineffective.

I suspect that a draft inducer would not, by design, create an overly strong draft in the chimney. Some draft inducers will operate at variable speeds which would allow you to create just enough draft in the chimney to allow you to prevent smoking. This would be a good choice in a tight home or one with a natural draft furnace.

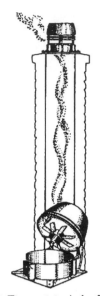

◆ **Figure 6-9.** *A draft-inducing fan for fireplaces.*
Courtesy: *Sleepy Hollow Chimney Supply, LTD.*

Wind-related Performance Problems

1. *Wind-induced downdrafts.*
   The surrounding landscape and the peak of the roof may direct wind down a chimney. Either raise the chimney above the downward path of the wind, or install a chimney cap that will divert the wind and in the process, create a negative pressure at the chimney termination. Since a chimney cap serves other useful functions, try this solution first. I don't recommend a chimney cap that rotates with the wind; moving parts can get covered with creosote and stick.

2. *Wind-Loading.*
   When wind strikes a building, it creates zones of high and low pressure. In some cases, the interior of the house can become so de-pressurized that it uses the chimney (and whatever gases are in it at the time) to equalize the pressure. The solution is to open a window on the windward side. Be sure openings on the other three sides of the building are closed, especially on the upper floors.

◆

Chapter 7
Combustion Theory:
What Happens in the Firebox

Understanding how wood burns and how your stove produces heat improves your control of a woodburning appliance. And with an eye on the weather, you can fine tune your stove to keep the house comfortable under a range of outdoor temperatures. Knowledge of solid fuel combustion will get you the most heat from your wood, keep wood stove emissions to a minimum, and reduce the risks of a chimney fire.

For fuel to burn, there must be a source of air, and sufficient heat for the fuel to reach its ignition temperature. As long as fuel, air, and enough heat are present, a fire, once started, is a self-perpetuating chemical reaction.

For the fire to consume all the fuel and provide clean combustion, the "three T's" are necessary: time, temperature, and turbulence.

During the combustion process, high temperatures cause the wood to release moisture, followed by the volatile gases. Oxygen in the air (about 21 percent by volume) is required to sustain the fire, while **turbulence** (the mixing of air with volatile gases and vapors) ensures complete combustion. To burn wood completely, this mixture requires a period of time at ignition temperatures.

In fireplaces and most wood stoves, combustion is incomplete because some volatile gases are sucked up the chimney before they have a chance to burn. The ability of an appliance to convert fuel into heat is referred to as its **combustion efficiency**.

What are these volatile gases? In firewood they are primarily carbon, oxygen, and hydrogen (hydrocarbons) which are locked into the cellulose and lignite of the wood as organic compounds. Because wood is geologically "young," these volatiles are easily driven out. They then combine with air and release heat and light. If combustion is complete, the carbon is converted to carbon dioxide (CO_2) and the hydrogen to water (H_2O). When one of the "three T's" is missing and combustion is incomplete, the by-products of combustion are carbon monoxide (CO), soot (C), free hydrogen (H_2), and numerous tars and other organic compounds.

THE THREE STAGES OF COMBUSTION

The burning of wood is a three-stage process. When a piece of wood first enters the firebox, it stays below the boiling point (212°F.) until the water has been driven out from deep inside the log and evaporated. When wood is either wet or green its moisture content can be more than 50 percent; even when air-dried it is still 20 percent. The more moisture in the wood, the more heat is needed for evaporation. As the water is driven off, there will be a hissing sound in the firebox.

At 300°–400°F. the wood begins to release the volatile gases. Some of these will burn; others will mix with the carbon dioxide and water vapor, be carried out of the fire zone, and appear at the top of the stack as smoke. At 400°F. the smoking ceases.

In the second stage of combustion, temperatures must reach 1,100°F. to burn all the gases, and this won't occur without sufficient oxygen. With the right amount of heat and air, the gases are forced into flame, producing heat and combustion efficiencies. The new piece of wood, or rather the gases just above it, burns to produce a yellow flame.

After the gases are burned off, the remaining charcoal burns in the third stage of the cycle. The charcoal contains almost half of the wood's heat potential. During this part of the burn cycle, there is little visible flame. Because the remaining fuel is more compact and because there is less surface area exposed to air, the rate of combustion is slower. Also, charcoal is a better thermal insulator than wood, and therefore exposes itself more slowly to the surface where combustion takes place.

This is important to remember because low stovepipe temperatures during this phase of combustion do not indicate incomplete combustion. They only indicate the need for more fuel if the fire is to be kept going.

When a fire is burning in a wood stove, several stages of combustion occur simultaneously, each at a specific place in the fire depending on the temperature and the oxygen present in that particular location. For complete combustion there must be an adequate mixing of the air and fuel at high temperatures.

During start-up and reloading, the burn is less clean because the combustion is less complete. At start-up, the inside temperature of the stove walls moderate the flames, and during reloading the addition of cooler air and fresh wood momentarily alter the combustion process. In both cases unburned volatiles escape up the venting system. Advanced stove design promotes cleaner combustion by a redesign of the firebox to re-radiate heat back into the fire. Insulation and/or firebrick has been added to combustion zones to help maintain gas-combustion temperatures. Air inlets have also been added to introduce pre-heated air at both the bottom and top of the fuel load. These inlets supply oxygen to high gas zones. In catalytic stoves, materials that lower the ignition temperature of the gases complete the combustion process.

The Energy Content of Wood

A **British thermal unit** (Btu) is the amount of energy required to raise the temperature of one pound of water, one degree Fahrenheit. Dry firewood contains about 8,600 Btus per pound; the gaseous component of wood accounts for over half of the available energy and the solid material contains the remainder.

The actual energy produced from a pound of wood depends upon the wood's moisture content and its chemical composition. The heating value of a particular species does not account for the energy required to evaporate the moisture. It is, however, the accepted standard and gives a more accurate reference when comparing efficiencies of different systems or fuels.

EMISSIONS

It is the incomplete combustion of hydrocarbons around which the issue of wood stove emissions revolves. Pollution from conventional wood stoves and its effect on air quality are the reasons we now have government regulations regarding woodburning. Wood is actually a clean fuel when seasoned and properly burned. It has a low sulfur content of .02 percent, whereas heating oil has a sulfur content of .2 percent; sulfur oxides form sulfuric acid which when mixed with water become acid rain.

Look at the top of your chimney. If you don't see anything coming out, you're burning cleanly. You may see what looks like white smoke which forms a foot above the chimney and seems to disappear. This is water vapor condensing and then evaporating. Anything else is unburned fuel, including carbon particles, resins, and tars, accompanied by an acrid, chemical smell. When this happens, you are not getting a clean burn.

Troubleshooting a Dirty Burn

If the problem isn't inherent in the system (poor stove design or a venting system that doesn't allow for sufficient turbulence in the firebox), check the fuel load. Is there only one large log on the fire? Is the fuel load tightly packed? These conditions are detrimental to the combustion process. It is possible to **bank** a fire (densely packed fuel load on a full, raked bed of coals) if: it's cold enough outside to create a strong enough draft in the venting system to provide the necessary turbulence, there is enough air for combustion, and the load is well seasoned. These factors are interrelated. The lower the moisture content of the wood load, the less air circulation is necessary and the more densely it can be packed. Also, fire can better tolerate wet wood if it is cut in smaller pieces since there is more surface area for that moisture to be driven from. It becomes a delicate balance. The presence of a catalytic combustor in the system helps this balance by burning gases at 500 — to 600°F. instead of the 1,000 to 1,200°F. normally required.

The most common cause of a dirty burn in pre-EPA stoves is inadequate combustion air. Complete combustion won't take place without *turbulence* in the firebox. Turbulence is caused by a draft in the venting system. The draft is created by hot gases including dilution air. The amount of dilution air required depends on the outside temperature, the venting system configuration, and the moisture content and size of the fuel load. Air is also needed to maintain a critical, minimum rate of combustion. The conscientious stove tender is constantly assessing the rate of combustion to meet heating needs while achieving a clean burn.

Can a fire get too much air? Yes. As the load of fuel ignites, the temperature of the venting system, firebox, and fuel load itself rises which accelerates the combustion process. If the supply air is allowed to remain in a full open position, the maximum firing rate for the stove can be exceeded and damage the stove. This is true for cordwood-burning metal stoves. The firing of a pellet stove is limited by the fuel which is fed into the combustion chamber at a controlled rate. The maximum rate of combustion is desirable in masonry heaters since the materials used are designed to withstand the hottest temperatures that can be reached in a wood fire.

Later in the book, there are scenarios of heating strategies that incorporate unattended woodburning. This practice should be done **only** after the stove has been operated under a variety of outside temperatures while attended and **with** a stovepipe thermometer to determine how the draft controls (air intakes) will affect the heat output of the stove. You may decide that your installation is not predictable enough to suit you and that you are not comfortable leaving the stove unattended. **Don't.** Heat is certainly important in cold weather but your peace of mind is more important. Let the heating system take over when you are not home.

Why does wood burn faster as it gets colder outside? The rate of combustion is affected by several factors including outside temperature — the colder the outside temperature, the more buoyant the hot gases in the chimney. This increases the draw or draft in the chimney which in turn increases the turbulence in the firebox and makes the house an inadvertent bellows. To compensate for this, it is preferable to reduce the air supply, or to install a barometric draft regulator. Cold weather is the time to burn the larger pieces of wood and mix in any green wood if supplies require it.

TIPS FOR CLEAN BURNING

1. *Use seasoned wood.*
   The importance of burning seasoned wood can't be overemphasized. The amount of water in your fuel influences how clean the burn. Don't rely on your wood supplier to season it for you. Have your wood supply split and stacked a year in advance—it is like having money in the bank; as it seasons its heat content increases.

2. *Insist on well-split wood.*
   Since the new stoves have smaller fireboxes, firewood dealers are splitting their wood into smaller pieces. Older stoves and wood furnaces take much bigger pieces and this means less processing for the dealer. Don't take bigger pieces than you asked for, even at a reduced price unless you're sure you want to buck and split them again yourself. Your delivery will have a variety of thicknesses. That's actually a help as part of the fine-tuning strategy. As a rule, you should be able to fit at least three average sized pieces in the stove at one time.

3. *Keep a supply of dry kindling on hand.*
   You will be tempted to reduce the air supply and keep a smoldering fire going when you don't need the heat, if you don't have some kindling stored.

4. *With new stoves, load enough fuel for a complete burn cycle.*
   Recent tests have shown that in the new low-emission stoves, frequent reloading pollutes more than letting a charge of fuel complete a burn cycle (only glowing coals remaining) before reloading.

Fine-Tuning Aids

1. Some fireboxes allow you to view the fire through glass in the door. This option lets you make sure that the fire is burning with a flame and not just smoldering. You can also see how vigorous the fire is and monitor the effects of reducing the air

◆

supply. Glass doors provide added enjoyment and the flickering flame complements reading and conversation.

2. A variety of thermometers are available; some sit on top of the stove, others attach to the stovepipe magnetically, while the "probe" type is inserted into a hole in the pipe to more accurately read flue gas temperatures. The important point is to calibrate the thermometer when you have a clean fire burning. That reading will be slightly different for each thermometer and for each place on the particular stove or pipe. Don't rely solely on the ranges given on the thermometer. You may discover that your installation requires a minimum reading that is in the middle or upper end of the "recommended range" on the dial.

    A stovetop thermometer is essential for catalytic stoves which must reach a "light-off" temperature for a given period before it can be engaged into the flue path, and the only way you can be sure you have followed this procedure correctly is to use a thermometer.

3. Massachussetts codes require that any stove without an internal damper have a stovepipe damper. A stovepipe damper is a round plate with small holes in it that pivots inside the stovepipe on a rod that is turned by the spiral handle at its end. Correctly installed, the plate will be at the same orientation as the handle. Proper use of the damper can enhance combustion. Older stoves that aren't airtight must have a stovepipe damper to control the fire.

    Stovepipe dampers also have a safety purpose. They limit the air supply to the chimney in the event of a chimney fire. In some situations where there is excessive draft, the stovepipe damper increases "residence time," i.e., it prevents volatile gases from being sucked out of the firebox before they have had time to ignite. At the end of the firing cycle of a fuel load, a nearly closed pipe damper will allow more heat from the burning coals to be transferred into the living space. The holes in the damper still allow gases to escape up the chimney.

◆

By "dampening" the fire down to a smolder, a stovepipe damper can clog a chimney with creosote. A clogged chimney is a fire hazard, and too high a price to pay for the little added convenience. If you think that the pipe damper holds heat, read the section on energy conservation in chapter 3.

Striving for high heat transfer efficiency by letting as little heat up the chimney as possible results in poor combustion efficiency. Remember that the combustion chamber and heat exchanger are essentially one and the same — a wood stove delivers the heat as it is produced.

EFFICIENT BURNING

The overall energy efficiency of a heating system is the product of the heat produced during combustion multiplied by the percentage of that heat that can be utilized.

$$\text{overall energy efficiency} = \frac{\text{useful heat energy output}}{\text{fuel energy input}}$$

Long runs of stovepipe and heat reclaimers improve overall efficiency in an unbaffled, non-airtight stove. However, they are not worth the cost or annoyance in a new wood stove installation. If you have sized your appliance for the space, they shouldn't be necessary. The new stoves are also designed to operate with a minimum draft, long runs of pipe can hamper draft below that minimum.

To reduce stove emissions and make wood heating more environmentally benign, stove manufacturers have improved both combustion efficiency and heat transfer efficiency. As a result the new certified wood stoves are capable of high overall energy efficiency. The stove's actual overall performance, however, is still determined by how willing the stove user is to allow the stove to do its job. Closing down the air supply too soon or too much achieves a longer burn, but the total heat output will be less than if there is always sufficient air for a clean burn.

Chapter 8
Fire Safety

As Black Elk once said, "This is the fire that will help the generation to come, if they use it in a sacred manner. But if they do not use it well, the fire will have the power to do them great harm." Although fire allows us to live comfortably in the winter, it can be a force of devastating destruction.

Is woodburning safe? Woodburning certainly can be done safely, but the hazards associated with woodburning emphasize the need for proper caution. You may already have a safe installation; if it isn't, it can be made safe. If you are adamant about not trusting a wood fire inside your house, there are residential wood heating systems that are housed outside and pump heated water into the home through insulated underground pipes. However, in my opinion, these systems sacrifice more in efficiency and emissions (they are exempt from EPA certification) than their margin of safety justifies.

Woodstove-related house fires are preventable. Aside from operator errors like forgetfulness — the loading door left ajar — or negligence — kindling left underneath the stove, fires usually result from ignoring safety standards. A thorough inspection of the installation can usually identify potential fire hazards and once the problem has been identified, it can be corrected. Since a wood stove installation or fireplace may have been in use for many years, temperatures as low as 90 degrees above ambient temperature, or 170°F., are sufficient for pyrolysis to occur. **Pyrolysis** is a chemical change, caused by heat, that occurs when flammable materials, such as a wood frame wall, are too close to a radiating heat source. These materials can become less fire-resistant over time and therefore increasingly prone to combustion.

The National Fire Prevention Association (NFPA) codebook #211 specifies clearances to combustible walls, floors, and ceilings; construction details for connections to chimneys and for hearths; and wall protectors for reducing these clearances. All stoves are sold with minimum clearances specified by the manufacturer. Remember, these are *minimum* clearances.

◆

BUILDING CODES

The buiding codes involve complex, sometimes politically sensitive issues. New materials and techniques must be continually evaluated. Issues of public health and safety, access for the handicapped, and indoor air pollution must sometimes be weighed against affordability and energy efficiency. State and local governments, and to a lesser extent the federal government, are responsible for making these tough decisions. ICBO, (UBC), BOCA, SBCCI, CABO and NFPA are all code writing agencies whose areas overlap geographically and topically. NFPA publishes a fire prevention code that is the basis for fire safety in many state and local building codes.

Clearances to Combustibles

The majority of wood-related fires result from exposure of a combustible component to enough heat for pyrolysis to occur; in building code terminology, this phenomenon is referred to as inadequate clearance to combustibles. The rate of pyrolysis can be very slow, but over time the combustible material undergoes a chemical reaction that lowers its flash point (the temperature at which a material will spontaneously combust when exposed to the air). This is literally a "time-bomb" situation. Ordinarily, a 2x4 needs to reach 500°F. before it will catch fire. Over time pyrolysis can lower the ignition temperature of that same 2x4 to 250°F.

Codes serve the important function (if followed) of ensuring that an installation has a generous safety margin. All new stoves are sold with a tag that specifies the clearances the manufacturer requires for that stove. If there is no tag, consult local building codes or the building inspector in your area.

Radiant stoves with no listing label should be installed at least 36 inches from a combustible wall or furniture. The connector pipe should be no closer than 18 inches. All residential heaters should be installed on an adequate hearth as specified by building codes or your building inspector.

We need stricter enforcement of our building codes to make sure this work is done right *the first time.* Sometimes it's impossible to inspect an installation adequately after it's in place. Critical areas get "buried" behind finished walls. The problem is that once the job is done, it is thought to be safe by the next homeowner. Building codes are minimum safety standards for chimney and fireplace construction and stove installation. They should be strictly enforced.

There are always unique installations that require interpretation of the codes. Ask your local building inspector if he will approve your installation *before* you start. He may have some useful advice pertaining to methods and materials. *Wood Heat Safety* by Jay W. Shelton (Garden Way Publishing, 1979) is a thorough reference for anyone who wishes to "do-it-yourself." This book also mentions methods and materials for solving particular installation problems.

If we look to Europe, especially to Denmark and Germany, there are models for safety that we in the USA would be wise to follow. They include better funding for the enforcement process, better qualified pesonnel, and prompt installation inspection so as not to hold up a phase of construction.

Perhaps also the insurance industry should take a more pro-active role by requiring specific safety inspections prior to writing insurance policies.

Wood Stove Installations

Whether you install your wood stove or have it done professionally, here are some guidelines.

1. Get a copy of the building codes that pertain to stove installations.
2. To determine the location of the stove, cut a piece of paper or cardboard to the dimensions of the stove. Move this around on the floor to get your measurements from combustible walls. (Drywall over wood framing is a combustible wall.)
3. If you will need a heat shield, it should be spaced out one inch from combustible surfaces (or from the stove) and open at top and bottom to allow air circulation. The heat shield can be 22 gauge steel and large enough to protect the stove from nearby combustibles. Consult your local building inspector.
4. For stoves vented into a masonry chimney, the sections of stovepipe connector should be secured with three screws and should slide through a thimble but not enter the flue itself.

"Snap-lock," 24 gauge pipe is adequate, but 22 gauge welded-seam pipe is a good value for the extra money.

The code specifies that stovepipe sections be attached with the crimped end going toward the stove and longitudinal joints facing upward. This allows the liquid creosote to be contained inside the pipe.

Double wall, insulated stovepipe is available for situations where single wall pipe won't meet required clearances.

5. Locate the stove so that no more than two elbows are required.

6. Use a "tee" instead of a 90-degree elbow, especially at the bottom of a vertical section. This gives you access to the inside of the connector for visual inspection and cleaning.

7. To ensure a tight fit between the connector pipe and the collar of your stove, use a piece of stove gasket "tape" which is a flat gasket that can be wrapped around the pipe as it is slid into the stove collar. Furnace and stove cement which are sometimes used become brittle and inevitably crack and need replacing every time the pipe is removed.

8. Your installation should be inspected. This will provide proof to your insurance company that any claim related to the wood stove was not the result of a faulty installation.

SAFETY CONSIDERATIONS

Multiple Venting Into One Flue

Although some states allow venting more than one appliance into the same flue, avoid it for the following reasons:

1. If a solid fuel appliance is burned improperly and soot or creosote is allowed to build up until there is not enough flue capacity, the exhaust gases may be diverted through the unused appliance into the living space. Such circumstances could cause asphyxiation and death.

2. In the event of a chimney fire, closing off the air intake to the stove, provided that the flue and clean-out door are tight, can deprive the fire of air and extinguish it. However, if other

appliances are vented into that flue, they provide another source of air to feed the chimney fire.

3. Natural draft appliances, including wood stoves, work best with a gas-tight flue. Good suction in the flue is necessary to bring air into the combustion chamber and create the turbulence necessary for clean combustion. If there is another appliance vented into the same flue, that flue is no longer "gas tight" and the draw effect of the chimney is reduced. It's much like drinking through a straw with a hole in it.

Chimney Inspection

There are definite indications of a weakness in the chimney. If you notice any one of these, stop using your system and contact your chimney sweep. Have your chimney thoroughly inspected to see if it is damaged or in need of repair.

Masonry Chimneys

1. *Cracks.*
   If you notice cracks in the chimney, have them repaired. Also have the chimney liner inspected for cracking or deterioration.

2. *Loose mortar or bricks.*
   Age, heat, or moisture can cause problems. In most cases, loose mortar or bricks indicate the need for a thorough inspection by a professional chimney sweep. The chimney probably is not safe, and repair or re-lining is necessary.

3. *Dark spots.*
   If there is noticeable discoloration on the outside of your chimney from the base to two feet below the top, you have a problem between the liner and the bricks. A dark spot or smoke stains are the result of a crack or hole in your chimney's liner, and creosote or smoke are escaping through the mortar to the bricks. If the problem is not corrected, a dangerous chimney fire could result. Consult a mason or a chimney sweep on how best to repair the damage.

Metal Chimneys

1. *Dents.*
   If a metal chimney is dented, replace that section immediately with a section of pipe of the same model and make.
2. *Dark spots.*
   If a dark or blue spot is noticeable, a weakness in or settling of the insulation in the pipe is probably the cause. Thorough inspection of the entire chimney and the replacement of the discolored sections is necessary.
3. *Warping of the inner liner.*
   The inner liner, if put under extreme stress, can warp and even separate from the rest of the chimney. Check the inside of your chimney periodically and have a chimney sweep clean and inspect it at least once a year.
4. *Clearances.*
   A two-inch clearance to any combustible material is absolutely necessary, unless otherwise stated by the manufacturer. A two-inch air space should be maintained from all walls, ceilings, roofs, and insulation. Numerous fires and deaths result every year because this rule has been disregarded.
5. *Metal chimney system.*
   Metal chimneys have many parts and are designed to be installed as a single, complete system. It is important to follow the manufacturer's instructions closely and to use all parts.

   Perform a smoke test before building a fire to test a new metal stack for gas tightness. Smoke candles are available for this purpose; they release quantities of smoke which can then be detected by visual inspection of the exterior of the chimney. Follow the directions that accompany the candles.

   An even better way to inspect the entire flue, inside and out, is to have the chimney video-scanned. Some sweeps offer this service; it is especially helpful for insurance purposes in determining flue damage from a chimney fire.

Safety Tips

- The thimble which connects the stovepipe to the chimney and will maintain the required clearances, is critical. If the chimney is behind a combustible wall, it is important to achieve the proper clearances to combustibles where the pipe passes through the wall. A UL-approved, **pre-fabricated thimble** or **wall-pass-thru** is used in these applications.

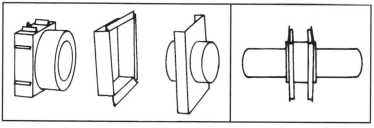

◆ Figure 8-1. *Ul approved thimble.*   ◆ Figure 8-2. *Ul approved wall-pass-thru.*

- Be sure the masonry chimney you vent into has a liner. It should also provide adequate draft. There should be only one appliance using the flue. Ask your chimney sweep to perform a smoke test to be sure that the chimney will contain combustion gases.
- Have your chimney cleaned and inspected at least once a year, preferably by a professional. Make sure the sweep is experienced, well-qualified, and has a good local reputation.
- If you are remodeling to accommodate a new stove, go to the building inspector's office and ask for a diagram of a typical code installation for your type of wood stove. Study the diagram. Also study the installation manual, and give it to the person doing the work. Make sure he meets or exceeds the distances recommended in the diagrams. Ask the building inspector to inspect the completed installation.

Before You Light Your First Fire

1. *Escape plan.*
   Assemble all the occupants of your house and discuss an escape plan. Have at least two alternate routes out of the house. If you live in the country, stash survival equipment in your car, particularly in cold weather — flashlights, sweaters, sleeping bags, blankets — plus an extra ignition key. Make sure that your smoke alarms (preferably one in each bedroom, as well as others in the main part of the house) and fire extinguishers are in working order.

2. *Fire drills.*
   Trigger your practice fire drill with a referee's whistle, or by setting off one of your smoke alarms. Some families hang a referee's whistle over the inside doorknob in every bedroom, to be used in case of an emergency.

   Meet at a predetermined location — by the car, under a big tree in the yard, etc. Avoid the possibility of anyone risking his or her life by going back into the house.

   After you have held several daytime drills, have a surprise drill at night — the time when most fires occur. Practice getting out fast. Race against the clock!

3. *Alarms.*
   Smoke alarms provide early detection and save lives. Battery-operated smoke alarms should be tested once a month. When you hear a chirping sound, replace the battery. If your smoke alarm is wired into the electrical system, it should "chirp" intermittently when the power is out.

   Chimney alarms are available that monitor flue gas temperatures and sound an alarm when a specified temperature is exceeded. The main benefit of these devices is that they warn the homeowner whenever the fire is too hot.

CHIMNEY FIRES

Chimney fires, like wood fires, need sufficient temperatures to ignite the creosote, and air to support combustion. Some chimney fires start part way up the flue. These are probably started by an ember, drawn up the flue and lodged against creosote on the flue wall. When the chimney fire starts in the thimble, the exhaust gases of a hot fire in the stove can reach the light-off temperature of the nearby creosote. Chimney fires can be caused by flames that lick up into a dirty connector pipe and spread into the flue. It is important to remember that once the chimney is clean, adequate flue temperatures will prevent creosote from forming. Creosote only forms when a slow combustion rate permits the flue walls to cool below the dew point of the gases. Water vapor mixed with volatile tars and particles condenses and coats the flue. This will happen with the cleanest burning stove if the fire is allowed to smolder flamelessly.

Chimney fires should be avoided at any costs. Some people say that they let the chimney fire do their cleaning for them, but chimney fires have burned down many houses and taken many lives. A hot fire may burn off creosote that has accumulated in the connector during the last slow burn, but the periodic hot or fast fire does not in itself keep the chimney clean. It is not an antidote, as is commonly believed for long, smoldering burns. The hot flue gases will help dry out creosote in the flue. Chemical cleaners also accomplish this, but if the creosote is baked onto the flue walls as a glaze, these measures can't be relied on to cause the creosote to fall to the bottom of the chimney. Once glazed creosote forms on the flue walls, it can only be removed by physically cleaning the stack. Or risking that a chimney fire will do it for you.

The temperatures inside a chimney can reach 2,100°F. during a chimney fire. If the house is old and wood framing members are touching the chimney (they rarely aren't), pyrolysis may easily occur. This means the framing members have a significantly reduced ignition temperature, and in the case of a chimney fire, enough heat could be conducted through the bricks to ignite that wood. If the chimney is not airtight, flames can also shoot through the cracks and ignite the building.

If the chimney suceeds in containing a fire, it may have been damaged in the process. During extreme heat, clay flue tiles expand, and the thermal shock may crack them. If this happens, the chimney's ability to contain gases is compromised and the damage should be repaired.

Fire Extinguishers

There are a variety of household fire extinguishers. Every household should have at least one.

There is a flare type of extinguisher which is put in the clean-out door or inside the stove for use in the event of a chimney fire. However, don't keep these on hand as a hedge against creosote build-up. You may not be around or you may be asleep when the chimney fire starts.

Teach Safety

Quotation from SNEWS, *Chimney Sweep News*. Jay Hensley, October, 1990:

"Thousands of children who have gone through practice fire drills, escape unharmed from burning school buildings every year. However, most children don't know what to do when a house catches on fire. They make deadly mistakes. They rush into smoke-filled hallways or down burning stairways. When you teach them the basics of fire safety and hold fire drills, small children have a better chance of escaping death or injury in a house fire.

Here are some of the most important facts children should learn:

- One match can burn down a house and kill you.
- Smoke can kill you, so get away from it fast. The air close to the floor is the safest for you to breathe. Since smoke rises, upstairs bedrooms are the worst places to be in case of fire, so you must get to fresh air quickly.
- Fire can spread through the house in minutes.
- If a door is hot when you touch it, don't open it — smoke or fire can rush in. Go out a window instead.
- When a house is on fire, **things** aren't important any more — **people** are.
- If your clothes catch fire, roll on the floor or roll up in a rug to extinguish the flames. **Don't** panic and run!

A game approach can make fire drills fun for small children. Children need to understand that fires can happen, but that people can get away from them. Then if a real fire comes, they are not as likely to become confused or paralyzed with fear. If children have taken part in home fire drills, they'll be better able to stay calm and get out safely and quickly. Young children can learn how to open a window, climb out, and go down a fire-escape ladder. Older children can go down hand-over-hand on a length of strong, knotted rope.

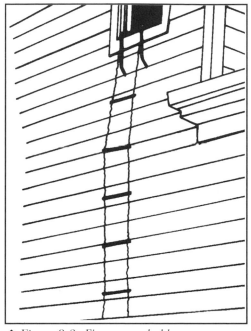

Stairways can fill up with heat and deadly smoke, so it's particularly important for upstairs rooms to have an escape route through a window.

◆ Figure 8-3. *Fire escape ladder.*
SNEWS, *Chimney Sweep News.*
Jay Hensley, October, 1990

Fire and smoke can engulf a house with terrifying speed. Fumes from burning synthetic wall/floor coverings and other modern home furnishings are particularly lethal. Never risk going back inside. Call the fire department from a neighbor's house."

Chapter 9
Stove Location and the House Heating Sytem

Most people interested in heating with wood want to get the most heat from their investment, but certain choices affect convenience and comfort as well as safety. This chapter looks at woodburning in terms of heating efficiency, convenience, and comfort.

In a conventional house, heating is a function of thermostat settings and heating zones. However, a wood stove establishes its own heating zone and influences the operation of your central heating system. Therefore, it is important to know where to locate it and how to integrate it into the existing heating scheme.

Let's imagine you just moved into a house and want to hook up your wood stove to an existing masonry chimney. If there's a furnace in the basement which uses the chimney, you need to know whether local building codes allow multi-appliance venting into the same flue. Maybe there is an unused flue in the chimney. It's important to know the physical condition and size of the flue you intend to use.

These issues are discussed in chapter 8 and will need to be resolved before you develop a wood stove/central heating strategy.

STOVE LOCATION

If the stove is to be located in a living space (rather than in a basement) you will benefit most if it is put in the space where you spend your evenings. If, for instance, you spend your evenings in the family room, put the wood stove there. If you don't, you may find that the stove's location *becomes* the family room, at least during the winter.

By being near your heat source, you benefit most from the heat it provides. In addition, it is nearby for ease of monitoring and loading and, of course, for watching the fire if the stove offers you that option.

The Thermostat

The closer the wood stove to the furnace thermostat, the greater its impact on the central heating system. If the stove heats the whole house you will get better heat distribution by opening all the interior house doors.

You may want the privacy of a closed door, or a little extra warmth in a bathroom. In either case, a portable space heater can do the job. There are electric-powered quartz and ceramic heaters that are efficient and appropriate for occasional use. If there is a larger space that isn't kept warm enough by the stove, consider a wall-mounted space heater which burns natural gas or propane and vents directly to the outside.

If the stove prevents the central heat from coming on, don't let plumbing on outside walls or in cold basements get cold enough to freeze. During the coldest spells, let the water drip in a suspect sink. For exposed pipes in the basement, install thermostatically regulated heat tapes.

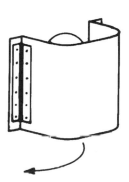

◆ Figure 9-1.
Thermostat shield.

If stove operation interferes with the heating needs in the rest of the house, insulate or shield the thermostat so that it is less affected by the stove. Fabricate a thermostat heat shield by designing a box that allows you access to the thermostat's controls yet shields the thermostat from the sight line to the stove.

If shielding the thermostat doesn't suffice, move it to a room that is more isolated from your stove installation.

HEAT DISTRIBUTION

A radiant stove heats the objects that it "sees." The objects then heat the air. If the stove has an outer jacket, much of the radiant energy is absorbed by this jacket which then heats the air. If you want to heat more than the space your stove "sees" a circulating stove may be a wise choice. To heat upstairs rooms, you will need to create a circulation loop (if one isn't already there) that not only allows heated air to rise, but

◆

cooler, heavier air to return downstairs. Otherwise, the heated air will hang around on the ceiling.

In one-story houses where the natural convection loop is flattened out, install a high speed fan in a doorway or mount one at the top of a wall.

Because warm air naturally rises, a radiant stove on the first floor is usually sufficient to heat a second floor. The floors are already warmed by the warm air mass the stove produces underneath them. And the combination of an open stairway and register(s) provide enough air circulation.

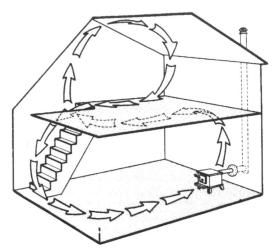

◆ Figure 9-2. *Air circulation patterns in a house heated with a stove. At the downstairs ceiling level, hot air moves away from the heat source.*

At the downstairs floor level, cooler air moves toward the heat source. There is a similar pattern upstairs, with warm air spreading out from the stairwell ceiling and returning along the floor to the stairwell.

◆ Figure 9-3. *Example of small quiet fan.*

What Is Feasible to Heat

It's difficult to estimate the space a single stove will heat without looking at a specific house. However, there definitely are limits — and guidelines.

If the stove is installed in a room with three outside walls, such as an addition or an enclosed porch, it should be sized for heating only that space.

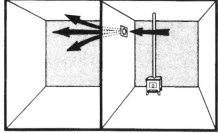

◆ Figure 9-4. *Small, very quiet fans can help distribute heat to other rooms unobtrusively. Typical dimensions are 4⅝ inches square by 1½ inches deep. Power consumption is usually 15-20 watts, and air flow is typically 50-100 cubic feet per minute.*

Figures 9-2, 9-3, & 9-4, courtesy of Solid Fuels Encyclopedia

◆

A corner room installation (two outside walls) in an older house with moderate insulation and original windows, will heat that room only. Enjoy the heat in that room and count on having a warm floor in the room above.

In most situations the wood stove may heat two or three rooms if there is: 1) some openness for radiation to affect heating, 2) there is a means for air to circulate naturally, or 3) you move warm air mechanically. Of course, the tighter your home's envelope, the evener the heat distribution. In many homes built to today's energy efficient standards, a single wood stove can heat a 2,000-square-foot home, with a supplemental heat source in the bathroom(s).

The Firing Cycle

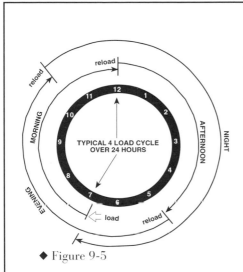

◆ Figure 9-5

Don't expect perfectly steady heat output from your stove. Wood burns best in cycles. A firing cycle is the time between the ignition of a fresh load of wood and its consumption to a coal bed. Each firing cycle should provide between four hours and eight hours of heating. Plan the cycles to match your household routine. For example, if someone is home all day, use four cycles: morning, noon, evening, and before bed. If the house is empty during the day, use three cycles: morning, late afternoon, and before bed. Adjust the amount of wood used for each cycle so that only enough coals are left to ignite the next load. Always load at least an hour before bed so you have time to flash the load before turning the air control down for an overnight burn.

Courtesy of John Gulland

The heat output of a typical wood stove has peaks and valleys depending on fueling. It is desirable to keep this output as steady as possible. This can be done by locating a heat-storing mass near the stove to absorb radiant energy and slowly release it to the space. Masonry walls and hearths serve this function to some extent. The thickness of either heat sink should be at least 8 inches. Use solid bricks or concrete blocks. Do not build the wall in contact with a wood frame wall; the masonry conducts heat and over time may create a dangerous situation. Refer to your local building code or NFPA 211 for the proper construction of hearths and masonry walls.

If you want "quicker" heat from your installation, a vertical heat shield behind the stove will circulate heated air into a room immediately. Also add curtains and weatherstripping to prevent heat loss. If the space is not continuously heated, install another heat source to provide instant heat. Natural gas and propane space heaters are generally a good choice here. They are easy to install and can be vented through an outside wall.

A circulating stove heats like a gravity hot air furnace. It is a wise choice for "chopped up" floor plans. The stove will produce lots of hot air which can be moved around with a fan or floor registers.

Wood stoves can make sleeping lofts oppressively warm. Install a ceiling fan to *de-stratify* the air. The big-bladed fans are a good choice if you also need them for summer cooling. If you don't, there are fans made for the purpose of de-stratifying warm air without the breeze associated with paddle fans. You can even install a **plenum** or duct with a fan to move the warm air into lower or adjacent spaces. If you have trouble distributing the heat evenly, consult a heating contractor for options that you may be unaware of. You don't need large ductwork or high c.f.m. (cubic feet per minute) fans to do the job. Some fans even operate on a thermostatically controlled switch.

Basement Wood Stove Installations

Why install a wood stove in the basement? Many people do for a number of reasons. The stove and associated mess are out of the living space. The floors are kept warm (a very compelling reason). You can hang a clothesline for "free" clothes' drying.

In a one-story house, a basement installation offers better heat distribution, but in general, a wood stove in an unused basement is a poor choice for two reasons.

◆

104

Firstly, the stove isn't as likely to be monitored and loaded at the appropriate times if it's always a trip down a flight of stairs. If the air intakes are left open, there may be no one nearby to respond to the danger of excessive heat.

Secondly, much of the heat produced does not benefit anyone upstairs. If you are aware of these disadvantages and still want a wood stove in your basement, you can compensate for the drawbacks.

You will need to wait fifteen minutes or more after stove loading to reduce the air supply (unless the stove has a thermostatic bi-metal damper to regulate the air supply). Either use a timer to remind you to make another trip or have an activity you can do in the basement to pass the time. Perhaps you create an exercise room there so that you can work out while stove-tending. In fact, treat the trip up and down the stairs as exercise! Do it vigorously, breathe deeply and feel good about all you are accomplishing in the process. The important thing is to have a *routine* and follow it rigorously.

To increase the heat upstairs, create a circular air flow between the floors. Return registers are best located underneath a window (north facing walls are best) and as far away as possible from hot air registers or an open stairway. If you can't get enough circulation, cut a register in the floor directly over the stove. A high-speed fan suspended under the register will increase the rate of circulation.

If the stove is near a concrete foundation wall, install a heat shield as you would to reduce clearances to combustibles. The heat shield will help keep radiant heat from being wicked to the outside.

Unless you have a dry basement, stovepipes will need frequent replacement and the stove will need more maintenance to prevent rusting.

Having done these things, you will still not reap the physical and psychological benefits of a hearth. Of course you could give in to its lure and finish off the basement.

SIZING THE STOVE

The size of the space also determines the stove's location.

A space that is less than ten feet in any dimension or less than 140 square feet will feel cramped with even a small wood stove. Sometimes a wall separating two small rooms can be removed or a doorway enlarged, to the stove's and everyone's benefit. To remove part or all

◆

of an adjoining wall will enable the stove to radiate heat more efficiently.

When you site a stove, remember that, in addition to the required clearances to combustible walls and furniture (usually 36 inches), 18 inches of hearth is needed in front of the loading door. Kindling and firewood should be placed a safe distance away.

If you aren't happy with the location of your present chimney, see chapter 6 for recommendations when installing a new one.

After you have determined the space to be heated and chosen an apppropriate heater, your lifestyle and the tightness of your house will determine the length of time during the heating season you can expect to heat that space in a clean burning mode.

LIFESTYLE

Depending on the weather and your house's heat load (the number of Btus required to maintain a comfortable indoor environment — usually 65° to 72°F. — on the coldest day of the year), the amount of wood heating you do depends on the amount of time you want to tend the fire. Many people don't light a fire until a predetermined date — for example, Thanksgiving — or whenever their local climate is cold enough to run the stove continuously without making the house uncomfortably warm.

If no one is at home much of the time and the occupants live with different or changing schedules, heating with wood will require you to adapt your lifestyle, or you will have problems. People are usually resistant to change, but if you are aware of this aspect of woodburning, you can prepare for the change. Remember, unlike conventional furnaces which cycle on only when the heating oil or gas is fed into the combustion chamber for immediate burning, a wood stove is batch-fed and relies on the user to make adjustments in the air supply to regulate the rate of combustion. The faster a house loses heat, the more frequently a batch-fed heater must be stoked to maintain a comfortable temperature.

Non-airtight wood stoves need more tending than their modern counterparts. Because they aren't airtight, they consume more fuel and require frequent reloading.

Successful wood heating requires an initial investment and an earnest desire to heat with wood.

Scenario 1

Suppose a couple (we'll call them Jason and Emelie) who both work, purchase a new EPA certified noncatalytic woodstove so they can make the most of the five acres of mixed hardwoods on their property. After having the chimney inspected for soundness and the woodstove installed to meet the local building codes, they are ready to "crank it up." Jason leaves for work at 7:30 a.m. so he gets the morning fire going good before he leaves. He sets the timer for 40 minutes and tells Emelie to close down the air intake when the timer goes off. Emelie doesn't have to leave for her job until 8:45 a.m. Jason is still getting a "feel" for the system and, since he knew his fuel load was still on the green side, decided to give the load an extra 10 minutes with the air intakes open and give the fire more time to drive the extra moisture out of the wood. Then he taped the "check the stove" note on the door before he left so that Emilie would be reminded to close down the air intake.

Emilie gets home first at around 4 in the afternoon so she takes care of the next firing; pulling the coals of the morning's fire to near the primary air intakes, and adding a fresh load of wood. Thirty minutes later the air intake is closed down again and the same routine is repeated before going to bed. During the heating season, Jason and Emilie learned that some adjustments to this routine would help make their house more comfortable. On days the weatherman predicted a warm, sunny day where the temperature might get up into the 40s, Jason would stir last night's coals as usual but instead of putting in a fuel load, would put in three small pieces and have a flash fire to "take the chill off." "The last time you loaded the stove and it got sunny and warm, it was stifling when I got home," Emilie said. She knows that if the weatherman is wrong, the thermostat is set at 60°F. and she can get the house up to 70°F. in the time it takes her to take a shower and change. He always tapes the note to the door, however. (In this scenario, good communication

(continued on the next page)

◆

is important. Not only for tuning the heating needs according to the weather but to insure that the morning's firing cycle gets completed. If there is ever any doubt that the air adjustment part of the cycle will not get done, then each firing cycle should be done by the same person.) By this time the flash fire is down to coals and closing the air intake will prevent the chimney from siphoning air out the house all day.

Jason and Emilie are realistic about how much heating they can expect to do with wood. They have found that with their lifestyles they can provide about 75% of their heating needs. During mild weather they use their stove in the evening only. (During the winter they heard about MassSave. In addition to getting their leaky front door weatherstripped, they received a complete computor-generated survey of conservation measures and practices and their corresponding average costs and payback periods. One of the recommendations was that they install a "set back" thermostat which could be programmed at different settings during a 24-hour period.) They set the thermostat at 60 for all but between 6:00 to 8:00 a.m. and 3:30 to 4:30 p.m. when it's programmed to bring the temperature up to 68°F.

Jason disconnected the stove pipe two weeks after they started burning to inspect for creosote buildup and again just before Christmas but there was less than a sixteenth of an inch of light brownish soot on the pipe. When the chimney sweep came in May, he removed only about a quart of light or " stage 1" creosote. Even though they could have stuck to the round the clock firings for more of the winter and saved some money on oil, their choice was the more fuel efficient one. During mild weather the draft in the chimney isn't as strong and they would have run the risk of the fire "losing momentum" - losing the flame that is necessary to burn gases and sustain draft by keeping sufficient heat in the chimney.

Scenario 2

Nancy and her two children have just moved in and her father gives her his old Riteway woodstove to help her save on the heating bills. She finally gets a load of wood delivered just before Thanksgiving. The driver says he dropped the trees last winter but just got around to bucking them up. Nancy isn't very excited about burning wood - one more chore to contend with. And she's nervous about the kids getting burned and the risk of a fire. It always seems she has a hard time getting a fire going so once she does, she keeps it loaded up so she won't have to restart a fire. And she never opens up the air intakes because she doesn't want to start a chimney fire. She doesn't like loading the stove either because every time she opens the loading door it "smokes up the house."

The second scenario has all the ingredients for a fire hazard and is not rare. When I encounter a "Nancy," who is afraid of fire, I listen carefully to her reply to my advice about the need for more combustion air so the fire burns hotter but cleaner and the risk of chimney fire is reduced. If I'm not convinced her fears are allayed, I suggest that some form of central heat would be more appropriate for her situation. To continue burning as she is not only increases the health risks from constant smoke spillage and the fire hazard from heavy creosote formation, its psychologically unhealthy to live constantly with something that invokes fear.

Scenario 3

Harry is a single professional who just purchased an electrically heated ranch with a fireplaced living room. His first year heating cost of $1,600 convinced him that he would rather heat with wood than watch an occasional open fire. At his stove dealer's advice he had a stainless steel liner installed in his chimney tieing directly to his newly installed fireplace insert.

During the fall Harry had a fire going soon after he arrived home and let it go out when he went to bed. Around mid-December he started loading the stove before bed so that he could awake to enough coals to revive a fire and have another charge of wood ready for another daytime, slow burn. By the end of February, he was back to the "evening only" fires. He was so pleased with the new electric bills though, that he nursed a fire along every weekend and enjoyed a toasty atmosphere during an otherwise damp, raw season.

Despite his having a "cold" chimney (on an outside wall), his chimney sweep informed him that his new, clean burning stove and matched venting system allowed him to follow a three firing/day regimen during mid-winter with only a light accumulation of soot in the chimney.

At the end of the winter, Harry figured his cost for electric heating, after factoring out non-heat uses at $400. He also used four cords of wood at $100/cord. After his annual chimney cleaning, Harry's heating costs were reduced by $725 over last winter's and he could expect his $2,000 investment to pay for itself in about four years. (This accounts for the interest he would have accumulated had he otherwise invested his money for that period.)

Scenario 4

Chris and Jenny were anxious to live a simple life close to the land. They purchased an old farmhouse in a very rural area. The earth beckoned them to start pruning and planting. Chris's carpentry skills and the couple's hard work transformed the old homestead into a cozy nest for their new addition, Megen.

The old oil furnace however was on its last legs and when nights started getting chilly, the young family decided they needed a more reliable source of heat. There being decidedly more ways in their neck of the woods to save money than to make it, they picked up an old, Glennwood cookstove from the farmer down the road who'd had it in his barn from he can't remember when. Chris took most of it apart (it was too heavy to move any other way!) cleaned it all up and, except for a little surface rust and a warped grate, it was in great condition — they had themselves a real beauty.

Rather than trust the old chimney, Chris installed a metal chimney next to it which would locate their new heater on an inside wall between the kitchen and living room (nice and close to that little, chilly bathroom). He carefully followed all the manufacturer's instructions and had the local building inspector o.k. the chimney and stove installation. He even built a handsome brick hearth and wall so that he could meet building code requirements.

Jenny had fun "keeping the fire" and found a good use for "recycling" Chris's wood scraps. Their stove not only kept them warm but met their cooking and baking needs and heated hot water for dishwashing as well. "Why did people ever stop using these?" mused Jenny. Chris mounted the roof every spring to do the chimney cleaning chore but creosote was always minimal and easy to remove. The stove's small and non-airtight firebox and Chris's lumber scraps all contributed to good combustion efficiency. And when they routed the gases via the bypass, around the oven

(continued on the next page)

section, the whole stove got hot which gave them good heat transfer efficiency.

Of course, the small firebox meant frequent loadings. About the time they grew tired of tending their stove through the night to stay warm, they heard about an interest deferred loan program administered by their regional Community Action Council which enabled them to replace their old furnace and the original windows that rattled every time the wind blew. Now they could get a full night's sleep!

Chris and Jenny could have used their loan money and opted for replacing the cookstove since it was their primary heat source. The old furnace was unreliable though and good sense prevailed: now they could go away during the winter and stay with family overnight without worrying about the plants, or worse yet, the pipes freezing at home. They knew that a new stove would be less polluting and would use less wood so they started saving up for one (which would complement the cookstove). In the meantime they had a very practical, safe and cozy hearth in their life.

As you can see from the above situations, successful wood heating requires an initial investment (or a "turn-key" woodstove installation) and an earnest desire to heat with wood. Both is all the better but the desire (or at least inclination) is essential. Since you are reading this book, you likely fit in here somewhere. The illustrations can show you in general the ways woodburning can fit into your scheme of things. I doubt there are two situations that are identical. You therefore have the opportunity to create for yourself a workable plan from the above samples.

WOOD SPECIES

A good way to control the heat output of a woodstove without compromising combustion efficiency is to burn the less dense species of firewood when the weather is moderate and the dense hardwoods

---

during the coldest weather. Remember, a stoveload of poplar has significantly less heating potential than the same stove loaded with ash or cherry. These lighter woods tend to burn faster so they needn't be split as small - unless you want quick heat. As always, moisture content should be in the seasoned range, 15% to 20% moist basis (see box below). Assuming your wood is all well seasoned (generally, the denser the species, the longer it takes to season) a given size stick of willow or alder will be noticeably lighter than the same size stick of locust. Once you have figured out the less dense species you will probably be able to pick it out of the pile from other species. Look for a distinctive bark or color.

Moisture content of firewood can be measured either by "moist basis" or "dry basis":

$$\text{moisture content (moist basis)} = \frac{\text{weight of moisture removed by baking}}{\text{initial weight of wood}}$$

$$\text{moisture content (dry basis)} = \frac{\text{weight of moisture removed by baking}}{\text{weight of oven-dry wood}}$$

Example: wood that is half water by weight has a moisture content of 50%, moist basis, but 100% moisture content by dry basis.

FUEL LOAD CONFIGURATION

As experience will tell you, it really makes a difference how your stoveload of fuel is arranged in the stove, how it will burn - or even *if* it will burn. A fire inside a stove is like a fireplace fire. It likes a loose arrangement of wood so that air can mingle with fuel.

The colder the weather and better the draft - and the looser packed the fuel load, the faster the wood will burn. When the slowest, clean-burn rate is desired arranging the fuel load more densely will achieve that.

The big chunks and rounds will likewise keep the hearth warm longer. Both strategies achieve this end by reducing the surface area of fuel to air.

Just be careful when you do this, that your wood is seasoned; otherwise your fire is smoldering and a lot of potential fuel ends up baked onto your chimney's flue, choking the flow of heavy gases and becoming a chimney fire "time bomb."

The trickiest time to successfully heat with wood is in the spring and fall. During these in-between months there can be large temperature swings in a 24-hour period. The sun is quite strong and an overnight frost can be followed by a 70°F. afternoon. If you are trying to maintain a continuous fire during this weather, you will most likely be: 1) producing hazardous glazed creosote in the chimney and polluting the air from a "damped-down" fire or 2) have the windows wide open during the day and feeding the stove a stick at a time, 3) be out of kindling or 4) tired of woodburning but not able to afford using your central unless, of course, you 5) don't have central heat.

If you choose a woodstove that is sized for the space it will heat, it will just heat this zone to a comfortable temperature during the coldest weather you experience. Especially if you live "up north" or in "snow country" that may mean a heating requirement of 50,000 Btus or more. But in the mild months you may only need to raise the temperature in the space 5°F. the morning after a chilly night — without keeping a fire overnight. The sun is now able to heat the entire building to 70°F. or more during the longer-than-winter day. A nighttime temperature that dips down to 30°F. doesn't have the same effect since the mass of the building has stored a significant amount of Btus which moderates inside temperatures.

That is why you find sunny spring mornings when you wait until around 10:00 a.m. to go outside only to discover that it is warmer outside than in. If you haven't turned the heat up or had a fire that morning, the building is lagging behind the relatively rapid solar-created outside temperatures. What's needed in this weather is quick response heat.

The Flash Fire Technique

A flash fire is a small amount of wood burned quickly. It is useful when you don't need much heat or when someone is available to tend the fire. The flash fire eliminates the smouldering fires that are common in spring and fall. To build a flash fire, rake the charcoal towards the air inlets and load at least three small pieces of wood on and behind it. The pieces should be stacked loosely in a crisscross arrangement. Open the air inlet to produce a bright, hot fire. The air supply can be reduced slightly as the fire progresses, but never enough to extinguish the flames. When only charcoal is left, the air supply can be reduced further to avoid cooling the coalbed.

Reprinted with permission from John Gulland, the May-June 1990 issue of *SNEWS, The Chimney Sweep News*, an independent trade magazine for chimney service professionals, PO Box 98, Wilmore, KY. Jay Hensley, editor/publisher.

Stoves are like houses in this respect. The more massive they are the longer they take to produce heat and the slower they respond to changes in firebox temperatures. In this respect, well insulated homes and masonry heaters are a good match in a northern climate. Both promote even inside temperatures regardless of outside weather.

SOLAR HEATING

If you are fortunate to have south facing windows you are realizing the gifts of free light and heat. Because windows also lose heat much faster than an insulated wall, they are best located on the south side of a house, east side windows are slightly better than west and north facing windows are the biggest heat losers. South facing windows provide the most passive solar gain when there is lots of mass to absorb and store the sun's radiant heat energy — like a concrete or stone floor and perhaps a short or "Trombe" wall.

A word of advice if you are planning on building a sunspace in a wood heated house. It is better not to locate the two in close proximity to each other. Sunny days will warm up the area of the sunspace and another radiant heat source is better located a distance away. More even heating will result.

Chapter 10
Wood Fuel

If your appliance is designed to burn wood, you will use kindling for starting the fire, and cordwood, cut to two or three inches less than the length of the combustion chamber.

KINDLING

The thin pieces of wood used to start a fire are called kindling. Some wood gatherers simply collect dead branches which they break up, often over the knee, and carry home. If you don't live close to woods or a park, don't despair! Kindling can be produced by re-splitting a straight-grained stick of split wood. Since this doesn't require the same force necessary to split a "round," it can be done on a porch or in a basement. If your woodpile is roofed and has a little extra space, re-split right there, leaving the messy stuff — bark, dirt, and dead insects behind. A 3- or 4-pound maulhead on a 12-inch handle is the best tool. The blades of camp hatchets are not squat nor heavy enough to do the job.

There are a number of kindling products on the market, such as fire-starters, "fatwood," and kindling candles. Kindling can also be found through commercial sources. Woodworking shops, lumber-yards, and builders create kindling as a by-product and are often anxious to get rid of it free or for a nominal charge.

If you have a local landfill, ask if they have pallets (the wood platforms many materials are shipped on) that you may have. Several caveats about using palletwood for kindling: It harbors lots of staples and/or nails. Be very careful when handling and cutting it. Wear gloves. A chainsaw, light enough to hold one-handed, will allow you to work without continually putting the saw down to brace your work for the next cut. Chainsaw only when you're fresh and for brief periods of time; it requires concentration and lots of bending over. There is nothing better than palletwood for mild weather burning when all you need is a "bloom" of heat, as my friend Fred Perry calls it. Throw a little on hot coals to revive a dying fire. You'll find it's the one stash of wood that you keep really dry. An excellent book on chainsaw use is *Barnacle Parp's Chainsaw Guide* by Walter Hill, Rodale Press, 1977.

WOOD SPECIES

I'm often asked what I think of apple wood in a furnace or pine wood in the fireplace. These questions are natural and I'm always happy to find woodburners with so much interest in the "how" of woodburning.

The critical issue here is wood *density*. All woods have about the same heat content when compared by weight. Wood is sold, however, by volume. Oak weighs about twice as much as the same sized piece of pine. Therefore, a cord of oak will have roughly twice the heat content. When buying firewood you get the most potential heat for your dollar with dense hardwoods. Some deciduous trees, or hardwoods, are actually lighter than some of the conifers, or softwoods. If you buy a load of cottonwood or aspen, you should pay less because it contains less heat content than the average load of mixed hardwoods. The resinous softwoods that leave more residue in a fireplace chimney, are completely safisfactory in the new wood stoves. Softwoods are preferred for starting a fire. They burn hot and fast. Of more immediate concern to a woodburner, is *the size* and *dryness* of the fuel.

If you cut your own firewood and have identified the tree you've just cut as a locust, remember what it looks like in cordwood form; save it for those windy, below zero nights. It's a dense, long burning species. Conversely, poplar, while still a deciduous tree and therefore a hardwood, is light and burns quickly. Use it during the "swing months" rather than the dead of winter. This kind of "fine tuning" makes woodburning an art.

A comparative heat content chart of different wood species has more pedantic than practical value. If you cut your own wood, you will be cutting accessible, dead, and/or unwanted trees. When choosing a stick of firewood for its heating ability, get to know how heavy a dry stick of wood of a certain size feels. Trust your tactile and visual sense also in determining how seasoned the piece of wood is. If there are numerous radial checks (cracks), and if the wood feels dry

Properties of Wood Species

Species	Energy Content* (million Btu/cord)	Species	Energy Content* (million Btu/cord)
Hardwoods		Honeylocust	28.3
Alder, red	17.6	Locust, black	29.6
Apple	..	Magnolia:	
Ash:		Cucumbertree	20.6
Black	21.0	Southern	21.4
Blue	24.9	Maple:	
Green	24.0	Bigleaf	20.6
Oregon	23.6	black	24.4
White	25.7	Red	23.1
Aspen:		Silver	20.1
Bigtooth	16.7	Sugar	27.0
Quaking	16.3	Oak, California black	..
Basswood, American	15.9	Oak, red:	
Beech, American	27.4	Black	26.1
Birch:		Cherrybark	29.1
Paper	23.6	Laurel	27.0
Sweet	27.9	Northern red	27.0
Yellow	26.6	Pin	27.0
Butternut	16.3	Scarlet	28.7
Cherry, black	21.4	Southern red	25.3
Chestnut, American	18.4	Water	27.0
Cottonwood:		Willow	29.6
Balsam poplar	14.6	Oak, white:	
Black	15.0	Bur	27.4
Eastern	17.1	Chestnut	28.3
Elm:		Live	37.7
American	21.4	Overcup	27.0
Cedar	..	Post	28.7
Rock	27.0	Swamp chestnut	28.7
Slippery	22.7	Swampy white	30.9
Hackberry	22.7	White	29.1
Hickory, pecan:		Sassafras	19.7
Bitternut	28.3	Sweetgum	22.3
Nutmeg	25.7	Sycamore, American	21.0
Pecan	28.3	Tanoak	27.4
Water	26.6	Tupelo:	
Hickory, true:		Black	21.4
Mockernut	30.9	Swamp	..
Pignut	32.1	Water	21.4
Red	..	Walnut, black	23.6
Sand	..	Willow, black	16.7
Shagbark	30.9	Yellow-poplar	18.0
Shellbark	29.6		

(continuued on next page)

Properties of Wood Species *(continued)*

Species	Energy Content* (million Btu/cord)	Species	Energy Content* (million Btu/cord)
Softwoods		Pine:	
Baldcypress	19.7	Eastern white	15.0
Cedar:		Jack	18.4
Alaska-	18.9	Loblolly	21.9
Atlantic white-	13.7	Lodgepole	17.6
Eastern red-	20.1	Longleaf	25.3
Incense-	15.9	Pitch	22.3
Northern white-	13.3	Pond	24.0
Port-Orford	18.4	Ponderosa	17.1
Western red-	13.7	Red	19.7
Douglas fir:		Sand	20.6
Coast	20.6	Shortleaf	21.9
Interior West	21.4	Slash	24.3
Interior North	20.6	Spruce	18.9
Interior South	19.7	Sugar	15.4
Fir:		Virginia	20.6
Balsam	15.4	Western white	16.3
California red	16.3	Redwood:	
Grand	15.9	Old-growth	17.1
Noble	16.7	Young-growth	15.0
Pacific silver	18.4	Spruce:	
Subalpine	13.7	Black	17.1
White	16.7	Engleman	15.0
Hemlock		Red	17.6
Eastern	17.1	Sitka	17.1
Mountain	19.3	White	17.1
Western	22.3	Tamarack	22.7
Larch, western	22.3		

* Higher heating value, assuming 80 cubic feet of solid wood per cord and 8,600 Btus per pound of oven-dry (zero moisture content) wood. In practice, values may vary at least 20 percent due to varying packing densities (the volume of solid wood per cord) and due to varying density of the wood. For very resinous woods, higher heating values are a few percents higher. Higher heating values per cord do not depend on moisture content except through the shrinkage of the wood as it dries. The values in this table are for 12 percent moisture content. A green cord would have a smaller heating value by a few percents.

Properties of wood species. Different common names are often used for the same species. Most fruit trees are not included in the above list. Most fruit wood is relatively dense, and is considered to be excellent fuel. Data from Forest Products Laboratory, Wood Handbook, Agricultural Handbook No. 72 (Washington, D.C.: U.S. Department of Agriculture, 1974).

◆ Figure 10-1 *(continued)*

to the touch and yet still is heavy, it is a dense species: a more concentrated fuel. A stoveload of this wood, burning at the same rate of combustion, will sustain a higher heat output over a longer period of time than a lighter, less dense species. Size, dryness, and fuel load configuration are the variables that will determine your choice of firewood on a daily basis.

If you are felling your own firewood, don't cut a shade tree. Don't cut a straight tree if you can cut a crooked one. Don't cut a healthy tree, if you can cut an unhealthy one. But don't pass up a birch that blew down in the last storm simply because it is birch and not, say, hickory. Burn the birch on a chilly day; keep a supply of hickory for the frigid ones. Don't bother with dead trees. They are rotten inside and have lost a lot of their heat content.

Seasoned Firewood

When a living tree is cut down, it is said to be **green**. It is easy to tell green wood from seasoned firewood. Besides feeling quite heavy, green wood still smells like a tree. Its bark is firmly attached and, if stripped off, reveals a green cambium layer between the bark and the sapwood. If you can get it to burn, green wood makes a sizzling sound and most of the heat produced will be evaporating the water.

Seasoned wood is decidedly lighter. It also has radial checks along the end grain and will make a resonant sound when struck against another seasoned stick. Very few commercial firewood dealers sell seasoned firewood; it takes lots of room to store and the wood must be handled twice. Most firewood dealers cut logs to length, split the rounds, and pile it into a waiting truck. The logs may have been "winter cut" but real drying doesn't happen until the wood is split open. Green wood is 50 percent water. Seasoned wood contains 20 percent water by weight. It takes 1050 Btus per pound to evaporate the water. These Btus can come from the sun which evaporates the water as the wood seasons. Or the Btus can come from the fire's heat. However, it makes no sense to use the fire's heat to evaporate water rather than to heat your home.

Emissions' tests of new stoves prove that moisture content is the most critical factor in achieving clean burns. Seasoned wood is essential to maintain high firebox temperatures to burn the volatile gases.

◆

Buying Firewood

Order your wood in late winter for the following season. This is the best time to buy your firewood for a number of reasons.

Buying early (before June 1) ensures that your firewood will be seasoned by the time you are into the coldest months of the year. As the wood seasons, its water content decreases and its heat content increases.

Ordering your wood early will also make your wood supplier happy! Your wood seller will appreciate your business during the traditionally slow time of year.

Firewood Delivery

To arrange for delivery, know the size of the truck that will be delivering and where you intend to have the wood unloaded. You want to save your back and minimize the distance between the woodpile and the wood stove. If possible, try to be at home when the truck arrives. It's a lot easier to decide where you want it than to move the whole pile by hand later.

A loaded cordwood truck can sink out of sight on an unfrozen lawn. Not to mention what your lawn will look like after the truck is towed out. If driving across a lawn is going to save you a lot of work, express your concerns to the supplier. Tell him to come when the ground is bone dry or frozen solid. He will understand. If he has to pay to get himself unstuck, he will have lost money on the sale and won't be happy.

Few firewood sellers stack their loads. Consequently you won't know if you have received a 128-cubic-foot cord until you stack it. The length times the height times the depth of the pile should equal 128 cubic feet. (The most common dimensions are 4'x4'x8'.) The pile will probably come out a bit less, but you should have more than 100 cubic feet. Random stacking causes less wood to occupy more space.

Another way to calculate the size of your pile is to ask the size of your dealer's truck bed. With a little quick multiplication, you can figure out roughly how many cubic feet were delivered. Deduct 20 percent for loosely stacked wood. If you find that, after stacking, you come up "shy," your wood dealer should make up the difference or give you a refund on the wood you didn't get. If face cords are sold in your area, be sure to agree on what is meant by a "cord" of wood.

◆

STACKING

After you have received your firewood, stack it for seasoning. If you leave it spread out on the ground, the bottom layer may grow some striking fungus but it will never dry. Covering a mound of wood with a tarp only traps ground moisture and ensures that *none* of it will dry. Stack your firewood off the ground on pallets or the equivalent.

There are different methods of stacking. If you stack outdoors, level the area as much as possible. If this is going to be a long-term stacking spot, spread a six-inch-thick bed of 1½-inch washed stone on the ground. This allows the bottom of the pile to breathe and keeps the wood from rotting. Or arrange a foundation of pallets. You'll need to cut these up, burn them, and replace the pallets annually so they don't become a rotting liability.

It's nice to have a tree, post, or store-bought cradle to stack wood against but it's not necessary. We managed for years to make a freestanding woodpile by cross-hatching the ends. Look for straight wood of the same thickness and split in half. Alternate the ends of each successive row until you have a fairly stable column. It is possible to stack up four or five feet before the pile gets precarious and difficult to reach. If your spot isn't level, don't try this method.

◆ Figure 10-2. *Cross-hatching woodpile.*

A few large, well-placed trees can support single rows of firewood. Such an arrangement isn't as handy as setting posts in the ground in the most convenient spot. If you can't set the posts securely, tie the tops together with rope to counter the spreading force of the wood.

Stacking Alone

If you don't have two-legged help, use two-wheeled help. A sturdy plywood-sided cart will prevent back strain. Position it between you and your destination and toss the sticks in. Do twenty minutes of this stacking each evening as a meditation or a way to unwind. You will be surprised at the therapeutic satisfaction derived from creating order out of disorder.

◆

Group Stacking

If you can round up enough hands to form a bucket brigade, stacking wood can go very rapidly and be a satisfying social event. You can pass the pieces along more easily if people face each other.

If you receive a firewood delivery in January, don't mix it in with the pile you're using. Leave it and stack it after the season is over or better, make two stacks — this year's and next.

There are many variations on these routines. Consider your building site and lifestyle to discover what works best for you. My friend Blake cuts firewood from around his property and uses a long meandering stack to border his driveway.

CUTTING YOUR OWN

If you intend to cut your own firewood you will need the following:

- chainsaw
- tools for adjusting the chain
- proper size diameter round file and flat file
- hard hat with eye and ear protection
- gloves
- work boots

A peavey or cant hook is helpful to roll heavy butt logs and support them while cutting (this is a two-person job).

WOOD STORAGE

Thoreau was right when he said that every man looks upon his woodpile with a certain affection. It's like looking at a winter's worth of warmth. Store your wood outdoors but as close to the stove as practical. Sometimes it's not possible or even desirable to store it all in one spot.

Two woodpiles allow you to get next winter's wood in after this winter's is stacked and ready to burn. Although most of us have a woodpile large enough for the coming winter, some wood species, notably oak, need a full year or more to season. With two woodpiles, you can rotate this year's wood closer to the house, garage, or basement, while next year's is stacked under a pine tree or wherever the delivery truck can dump it that is out of the way.

———◆———

To season next year's pile, choose a spot where air will circulate around it. This is more important than keeping the rain off. Ideally, keep the top of the pile dry but don't cover the sides. Corrugated metal roofing works best for this. Tarps blow off the pile or cover it up too completely.

My neighbor Bob, makes his woodpile of the same dimensions as his tarp. He then ties water-filled gallon jugs to the tarp grommets to keep them in place.

Woodsheds

Woodsheds are the ultimate amenity for the care and seasoning of firewood. The main advantage of a shed is that you can retrieve your wood without uncovering and re-covering the pile. Woodsheds can be freestanding or simply a shed roof extending out from the house. Our shed roof extends over our back door so that we can get to the wood and still stay dry. The ground is dry too, so we don't track in snow or mud. One open side works well as long as the wood is going to be there long enough to season, or has been rotated in from the "seasoning" pile.

One woodshed design is much like an Appalachian Mountain Club lean-to. The advantage of this three-sided shed is that its walls support the stacks. You can improve the ventilation by leaving an

◆ Figure 10-3. *House designed with integral woodshed.*

open triangular area just under the roof at the gable ends. Either overhang the roof or put in louvered vents so snow doesn't blow in.

This arrangement allows you to rotate the pile, which is especially convenient if you are cutting live trees and stacking as you go. Load from the back, filling the front first. At burning time your driest wood will be the most accessible. Any wood left at the end of the season can either be shuttled up to the front or left there, thus making the back into the front.

Size the shed so that it can hold a winter's worth of wood. Plenty of roof overhang will help you get the most coverage for the wall area and a covered place to stack or retrieve wood from a full shed. The overhang will also allow you to leave the top foot or so of the side walls open without letting in rain.

Problem: No exterior door near the hearth.

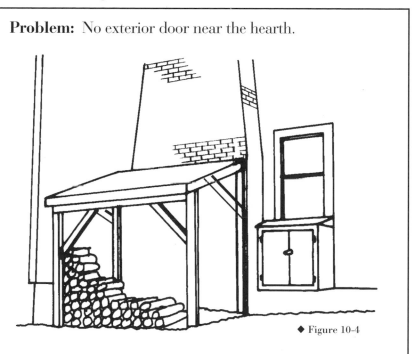

◆ Figure 10-4

Solution: One way to eliminate bringing firewood and its associated mess through the house is to cut a rectangular hole in an exterior wall adjacent to your stove or fireplace and build in a woodbox with doors on both the outside and inside of the house. Locate the woodpile near the wood box and easily accessible to your wood delivery area.

Indoor Wood Storage

Empty garages work well. Basements can hold lots of wood and are convenient for stoves or furnaces located there. However, be careful about storing unseasoned wood in such spaces because your firewood may also be home to carpenter ants, powder post beetles, and other unwanted guests. If the wood was dead when cut, keep it away from the house and out of garages and basements. These places work best as limited, covered supplies of stove-ready wood.

Chapter 11
Wood Stove Use

It is easier to start a fire in a wood stove than in a fireplace; therefore if you are a beginner, a wood stove is a good place to start.

A Simple Draft Test

Before laying a fire, determine how well the chimney is drawing. Blow out a match and hold it in the firebox. If the chimney is drawing, the smoke will rise out the connector pipe. If there's a flow reversal, the smoke will enter the room. This is a temporary condition or a "slow start" chimney. In either case, insert a twisted piece of newspaper up into the flue and light it. It will probably create enough heat to "prime the pump."

LAYING A FIRE

Newspaper is the standard fire starting material. Four or five pieces should be sufficient. Ball them up in the firebox near the air supply. Next, lay finger-sized sticks or the equivalent over the paper. On top add three or four wrist-sized pieces of wood. Arrange them so that air can circulate around them. If you use round sticks, select curving or gnarly ones that won't roll and inhibit combustion after the finger-sized sticks burn into charcoal and no longer provide support. Fit some shorter lengths across the shorter dimension of the firebox to construct a cross-hatched cribbing.

A traditional method for starting fires outdoors is to erect a miniature tepee. This method doesn't work as well in wood stove fireboxes as in fireplaces because there is not enough room. However, there is a variation of the tepee that works well if you have lots of short "wrist-wood." Start with the twisted up newspaper and some finger-sized kindling. Next lean the wrist-sized pieces diagonally against the back wall of the stove. This method works well enough so that if your wrist-wood is *dry*, the newspaper alone can ignite it. Lay the fire so that air can circulate around and beneath the bigger pieces until they are well ignited.

◆

Have the air intake wide open or, even better, leave the loading door open a half inch or so. In three or four minutes open the door to rearrange the fuel load and add two larger sticks to the fire, which by now should be forming coals. Close the door. It will heat up the stove and venting system, and build momentum that will sustain combustion of the first full charge of wood. In fifteen or twenty minutes, the last two sticks will be on fire. Now there are enough coals from the wrist wood to support a full charge of wood. If you have a supply of pallet wood or well-seasoned wrist-wood the procedure may take as little as fifteen minutes. If not, you can spend the better part of an hour nursing along a sizzling, wimpy fire.

CHIMNEY CLEANING

Chimney cleaning is a dirty, frustrating process, and reconnecting stovepipe will try your patience; it never goes together as easily as it comes apart.

If you can't see daylight when looking up through the vent hole or "thimble with a mirror," your chimney has a bend in it — or a blockage. Have the chimney cleaned by a professional to be sure that a chimney brush will go through the entire length of the stack. In fact, I recommend starting off with a professional cleaning, in any case. A certified sweep can quickly spot any potential fire hazards as well as show you a good approach to your chimney top if it is easier to clean from above. If possible, watch the sweep. You will pick up tips that can save you time and aggravation. Ask the sweep what size of brush he is using. It will save you a trip up to the top of the chimney. Of course, if that is the only way you can run a brush up and down the flue, you might as well make the trip. It may give you a sense of whether or not you will feel comfortable doing it on a regular basis. If the chimney has been used for woodburning before, the sweep can tell you whether you are inheriting someone's creosote-glazed chimney problem.

Leave fireplace chimney cleaning to a professional. Special tools are required to clean and remove soot from the smoke chamber and smoke shelf. A powerful vacuum designed for dust collection will keep airborne soot from settling on everything in the living room.

The vents for fireplace inserts and hearth stoves should also be cleaned professionally unless the stack has a liner that runs through the entire chimney.

To maintain your venting system, you should be able to take the connector pipe apart, preferably at the thimble, to inspect periodically for creosote build-up. Some of my customers clean their stacks in the summer and have me come once in the middle of the heating season. Or we clean in alternate years if it is decided that an annual cleaning is sufficient; they still have the peace of mind of having a professional cleaning but cut the cost in half by taking part.

When to Clean

Check the flue at the thimble. If you can easily scrape off ¼ inch or more of creosote, or if the creosote is hard and difficult to scrape off, it's time to clean the stack.

Glazed Creosote

If you operate the stove properly and it is correctly sized, you shouldn't find hard-to-remove, glazed creosote — at least not in the thimble. You may discover a thin layer at the top of the chimney where the condensation of gases is most likely to occur. This should be removed with a hand scraper. If you find glazed creosote, your brush will not remove it. Call a sweep.

How to Clean Your Stack

To clean your chimney, you will need:
- dust mask
- sock hat
- gloves
- screwdriver or small visegrips (for taking the pipe apart)
- wirebrush (preferably with an attached paint scraper)
- a bucket and shovel
- a mirror
- a book of matches
- a powerful flashlight
- a chimney brush
- preferably enough screw-together fiberglass rods to run the length of the flue or
- a long rope and a helper

Start at the clean-out. Cover the floor with a dropcloth or newspapers. Cover the floor under the thimble and stovepipe. If you don't have a clean-out door, have a sweep or mason install one. Remove any debris and creosote that have fallen to the bottom. You may also find leaves, dead birds, or a nest. If you don't have a chimney cap with screening around the sides, it's time to buy one. Once the debris in the clean-out is removed, you will know how much material you have removed during your brushing. If the chimney is straight, shine the mirror up the flue to see roughly how coated the flue is. If you don't see a clean flue outline framing the sky, lower your bare rods down the flue and flail them around inside to remove any large, loose chunks. Wear the dust mask and hat, and if possible, position yourself upwind of the chimney. Otherwise, the brush may cause falling creosote to form a plug part way down the chimney. If the rods don't bang around inside the flue when flailing, leave them in the flue. Go down to the clean-out and attach the brush to the rods. (Be sure you send down the "female" end of the rod that will screw onto the brush.) Return to the roof. Your first brushing will be from the bottom up.

Make sure the clean-out and stove loading doors are closed before going up on the roof. At this point be patient, deliberate, and totally "in the moment." As you push or pull the brush through the flue, listen for the sound of creosote falling to the bottom of the chimney. Proceed until you are satisfied that your brush has done all it can.

Now remove and clean the connector pipe and thimble hole. If the connector is longer than three feet, remove it in two pieces. Wiggle the pipe to see if there is a loose joint (if you have two elbows, find a joint between them). Before you start to unscrew, scratch a mark across the joint of the two sections being separated; it will help you reassemble it. Knock any loose soot into a bucket and carry the pipe outside for cleaning with the wirebrush. The scraper will come in handy for gritty deposits.

Take your light and position it so that it illuminates the thimble hole while you work. This area gets more build-up because smoke cools as it enters the masonry. Reach through the hole into the flue just above. There may be deposits there which can be chipped away with a small hammer, screwdriver, or old wood chisel you have decided to sacrifice for this job. Wear gloves! The flue visible through the thimble hole should show brush marks and some bare tile. If there

◆

is a bend in the flue, check the draft with a match to be sure you haven't left a creosote plug above the thimble. The smoke from a blown-out match held inside the thimble should get sucked up the flue or out into the room (if there's a downdraft or you have a flow reversal).

Also clean the soot that is only accessible through the exposed stove collar. This may be your access to the combustor, if you have one. Before proceeding, take a minute to review your stove owner's manual. Inspect the combustor and remove any fly ash by vacuuming gently. Now replace the cleaned thimble and connector unless they obstruct your access to the clean-out.

The clean-out door allows you to remove the debris you have brushed out of the flue. If you remove more than two gallons, you should clean more frequently in the future.

If you use a rope with the brush to clean your chimney, take precautions against getting soot all over yourself when pulling the rope down from either the cleanout or the thimble. Stuff some fiberglass insulation in the cleanout or thimble hole around your rope to minimize the mess. Take your mirror and look up again. Isn't it nice to see a clean stack?

Ash Removal

The ashes must be removed periodically from a wood stove or fireplace. They contain an abundance of potash and trace minerals that are good for the soil.

Always exercise caution when removing ashes. In a pile they can remain hot enough for days to ignite a fire. Use a heavy metal container for the ashes and take them immediately outdoors.

WOOD STOVE MAINTENANCE

Each year the stove should be cleaned out. Use a light to inspect for warped or cracked parts. Some stoves have interior parts that can be removed for access to air channels and smoke paths. These can fill up with ashes and should be cleaned.

In catalytic stoves, inspect and clean the combustor as specified by the operator's manual. Fly ash can build up and block off the grid. Also check for damage or deterioration of the unit.

If the stove and connector pipe are located in a high humidity environment, coat them with a rust inhibiting oil like WD-40.

Doors that have gaskets should be checked. Insert a dollar bill between the door and stove. Close the door and try to pull the bill out. If you can, check the latch mechanism. It can be adjusted to make the door close tighter. Check also that the door is an equal distance from the stove around its perimeter. If not, it is warped and should be replaced.

Smoke Spillage

I have been told by customers that they had to give up woodburning because someone in the house had allergies or a respiratory ailment. This is unfortunate because there are always means for preventing smoke from entering the living space.

This is most likely to occur when the door is opened for reloading. Before opening the door, be sure that any baffles or pipe damper are in the open position. Open the door just enough, one half to one inch, to cause the fire to burn more vigorously which will, in turn, increase draft in the flue. Unless only a coal bed is left, you should hear air rush into the stove after ten or fifteen seconds. Slowly open the door enough to reload, watching the top edge of the opening for smoke spillage.

If you can't keep smoke going up the chimney following this procedure, some steps will be necessary to improve the venting system. This may mean raising the height of the chimney, upgrading it by installing an insulated liner, or by installing a new metal chimney. An experienced chimney sweep can help you determine the most effective course of action.

Chapter 12
Fireplaces Still Have a Place

My first experience in heating with wood was with an open fireplace in a drafty old house in Stamford, Vermont. My housemates and I were marginally employed, which was a good thing because we had to spend so much of our time cutting and stacking firewood. As a result of the Arab Oil Embargo the previous year, we had resolved to produce our own heat; we couldn't have chosen a more difficult way. The comfort zone on those near zero nights was a four-foot area in front of the fireplace.

It was a hard lesson to learn. Although I enjoyed the wood cutting and gathering and the satisfaction of providing for myself, there was little warmth for my efforts. This is probably what motivated the British loyalist Sir Benjamin Thompson, Count Rumford, to devise an efficient fireplace design.

Count Rumford was both clever and practical. After studying the insulating qualities of different materials, he designed a warmer uniform for the British troops. He coined the term "radiant heat" and said, "One must remember it is the room that heats the air, and not the air that heats the room" — at least until the arrival of the hot air furnace.

The Rumford fireplace design was never adopted in this country. In fact, it was not until recently that I came to appreciate the vast improvement of a Rumford over the typical "ornamental" fireplaces that are built in this country every day. It is curious that for nearly 200 years there has existed a design for a heating fireplace that has been forsaken for the "atmospheric" fire-viewing version which allows over 90 percent of the heat to go right up the chimney.

FIREPLACE EFFICIENCY

Compared to any closed combustion appliance (one that controls the burn rate by regulating intake air), the open fireplace is not fuel efficient. But fireplaces can be more, or less, efficient depending on their design and location.

◆

It is impossible to calculate an exact efficiency rating of a specific fireplace design because of factors that are unique to each installation. If the chimney is located inside the building envelope, the masonry mass will increase the heat transfer and therefore the overall efficiency. How well the damper seals when it is closed will also affect efficiency. A typical interior fireplace may be 5 to 10 percent efficient, while the same fireplace of Rumford design would be 30 percent efficient. The increase in efficiency is caused by the longer slope of the back wall of the Rumford firebox. The back enhances combustion by providing the smoke path with a hot surface to radiate the gases and more residence time for the volatile gases to burn. This results in a cleaner fire.

Table 1
Rumford Fireplace Dimensions [a,b]

Finished Fireplace Opening						Rough Brick Work					Flue	Angle	Throat and Smoke Shelf		
A	B	C	D	E	F[c]	G	H	I[c]	J	K	L × M	N	Q	P	R
36	32	16	16	16	28	4	44	19½	27	14	12 × 16	A-48	4	12	10
40	32	16	16	16	28	4	48	19½	29	16	16 × 16	A-48	4	12	14
40	37	16	16	16	33	4	48	19½	29	16	16 × 16	A-48	4	12	14
40	40	20	20	20	32	4	48	23½	29	16	16 × 16	A-48	4	12	14
48	37	16	16	16	33	4	56	19½	36	18	16 × 20	B-60	4	12	14
48	40	20	20	20	32	4	56	23½	36	18	16 × 20	B-60	4	12	14
48	48	20	20	20	40	4	56	23½	36	18	20 × 20	B-60	4	12	16
54	40	20	20	20	32	4	66	23½	45	23	20 × 20	B-72	4	12	16
54	48	20	20	20	40	4	66	23½	45	23	20 × 20	B-72	4	12	16
54	54	20	20	20	46	4	66	23½	42	21	20 × 24	B-72	4	12	16
60	48	20	20	20	40	4	72	23½	45	24	20 × 24	B-72	4	12	16

[a]These are approximate dimensions based on historical data of Rumford fireplace construction. As is true with all fireplaces, successful performance is experimental.
[b]These dimensions have been developed from the following formulas. These formulas may also be used for opening dimensions other than those listed. Minimum dimensions are taken from the CABO One and Two-Family Dwelling Code, 1986 Edition.

NOTES TO TABLE 1

A = Fireplace opening width, in.
B = Fireplace opening height, in. where: $2/3 A < B \leq A$
C = D = E where: $1/3 B \leq C \leq 1/2 B$
F = B − E + P where: P = 12 in. minimum
G = 4 in.
H = A + 8 in. for: $A \leq 48$ in.; A + 12 in. for A > 48 in.
I = C + 3½ in. minimum when fire brick are laid as shiners or C + 5½ in. when fire brick or common brick are laid as stretchers.
J = K/u, where: $0.50 \leq u \leq 0.58$
K = 1/2 (H − M)
$L \times M > 0.16 (A \times B)$

N = A = 3 × 3 × 3/16 in. angle (number denotes length, in.)
    B = 3½ × 3 × 1/4 in. angle
O = Nominal brick thickness
P = 12 in. minimum
Q = 8 in. minimum when A × B < 864 in^2; 12 in. minimum when A × B ≥ 864 in^2
R = Smoke shelf width (flue opening, in.)
S = 8 in. minimum when fire brick lining is used; 10 in. minimum when common brick lining is used.
T = 16 in. minimum when A × B < 864 in^2; 20 in. minimum when A × B ≥ 864 in^2

[c]Minimum dimensions

◆ Figure 12-1

Brick Institute of America

Perhaps a design standard should be adopted for fireboxes and smoke chambers that would incorporate efficient fireplace principles, i.e., Rumford dimension ratios; a smooth insulated throat-to-flue transition; an optimum diameter round, insulated flue; and an insulated firebox.

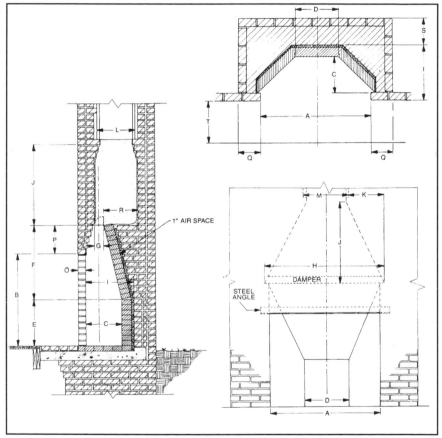

◆ Figure 12-2. *Rumford Fireplace.*

PRE-FABRICATED FIREPLACES

There are a growing number of pre-fabricated fireplaces on the market; some are designed for energy efficiency and some are as inefficient as their masonry counterparts. The ones designed for efficiency have glass doors to reduce the excess amount of air lost up the chimney, and have a provision for circulating warm air. Some consist of a metal firebox-damper-air chamber that is enclosed and faced with masonry. Most are pre-fabricated, zero-clearance units (designed with tabs or spacers to keep wood framing the required distance from the unit). They use a pre-fabricated chimney system that can be installed, framed in, and finished by a carpenter — no masonry skills are required.

If you are choosing a fireplace, are primarily interested in its ambiance, and are concerned about cost, you will probably look at pre-fab fireplaces. They come in a variety of shapes, sizes, and finishes. The circulator models, because of their increased efficiencies, are worthwhile options for anything more than occasional use.

Some pre-fabricated fireplaces have efficiency and emmision ratings which equal those of many new stoves. In fact, the ones that are designed to operate with the doors closed and whose combustion air can be regulated, are classified as stoves. These units must be installed according to the manufacturer's instructions. Pre-fab heating fireplaces, because they do not require the labor of site-building by a mason, are being specified in new construction because they offer real heating value.

Pre-fabricated fireplaces are a natural choice for condominiums and other multi-story dwellings because they don't require their own foundation.

I will admit my bias for the masonry fireplace. I have installed and serviced both masonry and pre-fab fireplaces and feel that, properly built both will give years of safe, reliable service. Like other appliances, fireplaces have a life expectancy. Masonry is a more elementally simple material than metal. What does this mean? When man-made things deteriorate, they break down or return to their basic elements. This is what happens when metal corrodes. The rate of deterioration of the material depends on how reactive it is with its environment. Metal is more reactive with heat and moisture than clay, fireclay and refractory cements.

Stainless steel has been used in some pre-fab fireplace units. Its high cost has limited its use. Remember that these units are only tested new and stress tested to meet the life of their warranty.

If you are building a new home, are you going to be concerned about the condition of the fireplace thirty years later? Many of these units have a thirty-year warranty on the fireplace and shorter ones on the chimney. Some are reaching this age, yet how often do we consider a fireplace worn out and in need of replacement? This is certainly something to consider if you own or are buying a home of this age with a "Prefab" fireplace. Routine annual cleaning and inspection for these units are essential.

FIREPLACE FURNACES

Fireplace furnaces incorporate a ducting system to distribute the heated air throughout the house. Some recirculate air and some bring in and circulate heated air from outside.

PRE-FABRICATED MASONRY FIREBOXES

To reduce labor costs and insure an efficient design, there are some new products that can be installed in new construction or used to replace deteriorated or rusted out fireboxes. These use modular, precast refractory units. Unlike the metal fireplace inserts that heat and circulate air, the masonry fireboxes feature excellent radiant heating qualities.

One unit, the Bellfire (Sleepy Hollow, Ltd., 85 Emjay Blvd., Brentwood, New York) is designed from findings in fluid dynamic research done by Dr. Rosin in 1939. The firebox is curving rather than angular. Rosin also discovered that the smoke shelf specified in Rumford's design did not divert downdrafts as it was intended to do, but actually created unwanted turbulence. This has been eliminated and the smoke chamber is streamlined into a "smokedome."

Both the smokedome and firebox are heavily insulated during installation to virtually eliminate heat transfer in these critical areas where maximum radiation back toward the fire (and into the living space) improves combustion and reduces emissions.

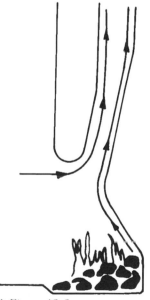

◆ Figure 12-3

Sleepy Hollow Chimney Supply, LTD

Recent tests conducted at OMNI Labs in Beaverton, Oregon, showed the Rosin fireplace reduced emissions by 50 percent over typical masonry fireplaces.)

MASONRY AIR-CIRCULATING FIREPLACES

A variation on the masonry fireplace is one that employs a metal air-circulating firebox. The assumption with such devices is that heat output is increased by the addition of heating quantities of air. Actually, the net heat output of this type of fireplace is probably no better than a masonry fireplace assuming both are located on the outside of the house. Located inside the house performance can be quite good depending on the sizing and placement of the air channels.

In any case, a metal firebox is a poor choice of materials for a combustion chamber. Firebrick stores and re-radiates heat. These characteristics provide an environment conducive to good combustion of the fire and good radiation, depending on the actual firebox configuration. Metal on the other hand, transfers and dissipates heat quickly. Flames are quenched and gases are cooled more readily against a metal surface so the radiant heat output and combustion efficiency is lower than with an equivalent masonry firebox.

The "Brick-o-Lator" is site-built, an all masonry, air-circulating fireplace which would provide the benefits of heated air without the problems associated with a metal firebox.

Some units heat air from outdoors rather than using floor-level inside air. This would seem a good idea but, in practice, has some problems. In severe climates, cold air can be drawn into the house when the fireplace is not in use. Also, condensation can occur on metal surfaces that are in contact with warmer air causing corrosion of the unit. Cold air entering behind an unused fireplace can make it feel like a freezer with the door left open.

In general, an insulated firebox of the Rosin design made of masonry is preferred; any heat transfer by convection taking place downstream of the combustion chamber.

GLASS DOORS

The most practical addition to any open fireplace is a glass door enclosure. Glass doors offer a number of advantages. If you like an unobstructed view of the fire and smoking is not a problem, leave them open until you are going to bed or whenever the fire is dying out. Glass doors that open all the way, unlike the more common bi-fold units, provide a less obstructed view of the fire. When closed the doors greatly reduce the tendency of the fire to de-pressurize the house and draw out heated air.

If you are a regular fireplace user, spend a little more than you think you can afford; a good set of doors will outlast the $100 chain store variety many times over. The curtain screens on any door will warp from the heat but can easily be replaced. I find the screens that open and close with a finger pull are less troublesome than the chain-operated variety.

To achieve anything approaching a good seal between the glass doors and the stone fireplace opening can be difficult. If the inside edge is flatter than the "face," "inside fit" glass doors can be custom made for your fireplace. Then fill the gaps with mortar but don't mortar them tightly; the metal will need to expand when it gets hot. Create an expansion joint using high temperature silicone and/or stove gasket "rope." Some people prefer the look of inside-fit doors, especially if they don't want to hide the fireplace facing or they want a more "integral" look.

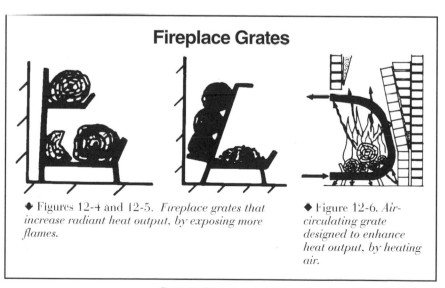

Fireplace Grates

◆ Figures 12-4 and 12-5. *Fireplace grates that increase radiant heat output, by exposing more flames.*

◆ Figure 12-6. *Air-circulating grate designed to enhance heat output, by heating air.*

Fireplace Technology In An Energy Conscious World, H. Morstead
Sleepy Hollow Chimney Supply, LTD.

INDOOR AIR QUALITY:
Fireplaces and Tight House Construction

To reduce heat loss and increase energy efficiency, we are building tighter homes. In a typical house built before 1970, the volume of air changed two or three times every hour. In colder climates, modern building practices have reduced that air change rate to once every two or more hours. One air change every two hours is the minimum recommended to maintain a healthy indoor environment without using mechanical means, such as an air-to-air heat exchanger.

Every vented appliance in today's home requires a constant supply of air while operating. Not only do the furnace, wood stove, and fireplace need air for combustion, but bathroom exhaust fans, range hoods, and clothes dryers also exhaust air from a building. Outside air must enter the house while these appliances are running or the building will de-pressurize. **De-pressurizing** occurs when the appliances' demand exceeds the house's ability to provide air. See Chapter Six, Figure 6-8.

There are hazards associated with tight house construction. Suppose the fire in your fireplace is dying down as you retire for the night. The house temperature is falling so the thermostat calls for heat. The furnace comes on, exhausting quantities of air that it needs for combustion. This creates a negative pressure in the building and because the windows and doors are well caulked and weatherstripped, pressure-equalizing air can be drawn down the still open chimney. This situation creates a serious health hazard.

Using Outside Air with Fireplaces

One solution to the problem of insufficient house air is to provide outside air for combustion. This is fine as long as the wind isn't blowing. When wind strikes a house, the windward side experiences positive pressure and the other three sides experience negative pressure in a phenomenon called **wind loading**. If the outside termination of the air duct, or **weatherhead**, is on one of these leeward sides, it can act as a chimney and draw air out of the house. If the weatherhead is on the windward side of the house, a strong wind can blow hot coals from a fireplace out into the room.

◆

House Pressurizing

If you don't want doors on your fireplace, and you want to guard against carbon monoxide (or smoke) contamination, keep the house under slight positive pressure. Use a small, high-speed fan to duct air in.

Using Outside Air with Wood Stoves

Some manufacturers have provided air kits that bring outside air directly into the stove. Outside air can also be drawn from the floor below through a register near the stove's air intake.

If you are concerned that the stove taxes the available fresh air, install a duct that takes air from a basement or other unheated space to a register near the appliance's air intake. This approach is less susceptible to the effects of wind, and easier to install than weatherheads.

However, because of the small air requirements of closed combustion appliances, there is no significant benefit to bringing in outside air.

Firelogs

Firelogs are a very environmentally sound alternative for fireplace use. They are made from recycled sawdust, bonded together by wax. A firelog burns much like a candle: the sawdust particles serve as the wick and wax is the fuel. In fact, the wax enables the log to burn at high enough temperatures for nearly complete combustion. Emissions tests at Shelton Research, Inc. showed significant reduction in particulate emissions, carbon monoxide and creosote accumulation, using firelogs when compared with burning wood.

APPENDIX A

Design Heat Load Worksheet

1. Client name: _____

2. Client address: _____

_____

3. Client telephone:_____

4. General dwelling description: _____

_____

_____

5. Outside design temp. (ODT), 97.5%_____

6. Volume of dwelling above grade: _____

*7. Average winter air changers per hour (ac/h): _____
   *See Figure 3-2.

8. Design temp. difference (DTD) = Dwelling temp. − ODT =

Transmission				
Surface	Area (sq.ft.) +	R-Value	=	Btu/°F. hr
	0.02 x volume x ac/h = 0.02 x _____ x _____ =			

Grand total = heat loss coefficient (HLC)

➡ Design heat load = HLC x DTD [_____]

◆ For an example of this form completed, see page 24.

The Journal of Light Construction
August, 1990, by Rick Karg.

Appendix B

Several studies have been conducted to monitor the effectiveness of the new stove technologies under "real world" conditions.

In one study conducted during two heating seasons (1985-86 and 1986-87), 68 homeowners in Waterbury, Vermont, and Glens Falls, New York, were provided with selected high-tech, non-catalytic stoves or asked to use their existing conventional stoves. The stoves were monitored for wood use, creosote accumulation in the chimney system, and particulate emissions.

In this study it proved difficult to assess a stove's performance because chimney systems, fuel characteristics, use practices, and stove maintenance produced a wide degree of variability in the data of any test sampling. However the study concluded that:

- The advanced technology stoves had lower creosote accumulation, wood use, and particulate emissions than the conventional stoves but, because the range of values was quite large, pinpointing causal factors was difficult.
- Creosote accumulation is strongly influenced by flue system type, and wood consumption was influenced by burning patterns and firebox size.
- Combustor durability varied.
- Some catalytic stove installations experienced condensation of moisture and organic material in the flue system, and subsequent drainage or leaching of condensate was a problem in some houses during very cold (-20°C.) weather. This appeared to be related to inappropriate installation and not necessarily to a limitation of the technology.
- Catalytic stoves showed variable performance and did not match expectations created under laboratory conditions.
- Add-on/retrofit catalytic devices did not perform well overall.

- Mean fuel-loading frequencies were identical for the low-emission and conventional stove groups, although the average non-catalytic stove fuel load was 56 percent that of the average conventional stove fuel load. This indicates that smaller firebox capacity (typically associated with low-emission stoves) does not necessarily mean more frequent fueling of the stove.
- User satisfaction was generally high with the non-catalytic stoves.

Two other field studies were conducted in the winter of 1986-87, one in Portland, Oregon, and the other in Canada at Whitehorse, Yukon. The three sites, including the site data from the Northeast, offered a good range of climates (4,800 heating degree days for Portland, 8,400 hdd for Glens Falls/Waterbury, and 11,600 hdd in Whitehorse) and a resulting range of burn rates. Average particulate emission rates for four technology groups in the three field studies are:

Catalytic stoves

Northeast	16.7 g/hr
Whitehorse	12.1 g/hr
Northwest	20.8 g/hr
Overall average	16.0 g/hr

Add-on/retrofit catalytic stoves

Northeast	16.9 g/hr
Whitehorse	16.2 g/hr
Northwest	14.1 g/hr
Overall range	16.3 g/hr

Non-catalytic low-emission stoves

Northeast	13.4 g/hr
Whitehorse	14.3 g/hr
Northwest	12.8 g/hr
Overall average	13.5 g/hr

Conventional stoves

Northeast	20.1 g/hr
Whitehorse	22.7 g/hr
Northwest	19.7 g/hr
Overall range	22.0 g/hr

In addition to this data, published by the EPA in a report entitled "Performance of Woodstoves under Field Conditions," the following observations were made:

- Many factors can affect particulate emission rates, but no single factor appears to be dominant in all stove types or models. In general it appears that stoves with smaller fireboxes, regardless of technology type, tend to have lower emission rates.
- Low-emission noncatalytic stoves, as a group, had the lowest average emissions. Overall, emissions measured

in the field averaged about twice the levels measured on these stove models during laboratory certification tests.

- Field emission levels on catalytic stoves exceeded the levels measured during laboratory certification tests by an order of magnitude ten times the observed laboratory results.

- Non-catalytic stoves, in general, had closer agreement between laboratory and field data than the catalytic stoves. This is thought to be because of the relatively low emissions which can result from a catalytic stove during laboratory testing: combustor temperatures are carefully monitored and not allowed to drop below the temperature at which they become inactive. In actual use, however, because of fuel loading and the lack of temperature monitoring by the operator, the combustors may be inactive for considerable periods of time.

These studies also dispelled the assumption, based on laboratory testing, that particulate emissions from conventional woodstoves averaged between 30 and 35 g/hr; the field study showed their average emission rate to be a full third better — 22 g/hr. Therefore, in order for the new generation of stoves to perform 75 percent better than conventional stoves, as the EPA had demanded, the new stoves would have to achieve an emission rate of 5.5 g/hr.

The studies acknowledged in passing that stove maintenance and fueling practices contributed to reduced emissions. What the studies didn't acknowledge was the contribution of the venting system to stove performance. The omission certainly appears to ignore the intimate chimney/wood stove relationship.

Anyone who has seen an existing masonry chimney venting wood smoke, before and after it has been relined to match the size of the woodstove outlet, can attest to the dramatic reduction in hazardous creosote accumulation. The liners, by matching the capacity of the appliance, optimize the draft. This improves performance and decreases creosote in the flue.

The most recent field test to date was conducted in Klamath Falls, Oregon, early in 1990. In this study venting systems were specified. Located at 4,800 feet above sea level, Klamath Falls had a severe pollution problem caused by widespread use of wood as the primary home heating fuel. The study was designed to compare the performance of 1990 EPA-certified woodstoves and to assess new stove durability.

The test involved three conventional wood stoves, three non-catalytic stoves and three catalytic stoves. These were all certified to 1990 EPA standards and vented into chimneys that were relined to match the stove collars of the appliances "in accordance with the appliance manufacturers' instructions."

The results of the Klamath Falls study showed a dramatic improvement in the performance of Phase II wood stoves over the earlier generations of low-emission stoves (Phase I) tested in the previous studies. The six certified stoves averaged 6 g/hr of PM emissions: "cleaner than any appliances tested in previous in-home studies."

The Klamath Falls study was funded by the Wood Heating Alliance, the national woodstove trade organization. The study demonstrated the viability of clean woodburning in advanced technology appliances, after considerable doubt had been cast by the ambiguity of earlier field studies.

In short, the cleanest woodburning currently possible is contingent upon a Phase II wood stove *vented into a venting system that matches in diameter the diameter of the stove's flue collar.*

Appendix C

EPA Certified Woodstoves
As of January 1999
Manfacturer Heat Output Range (Btu/hr)

Appalachian Stove & Fabricators, Inc.
329 Emma Road
Asheville, NC 28806
(828) 253-0164

> *Catalytic models*
> *8,400-29,100 (Btu/hr)*

Country Flame
1200 Industrial Park Drive
Mt. Vernon, MO 65712
(417) 466-7161

> *Catalytic models*
> *8,000-55,500 (Btu/hr)*

> *Non-catalytic models*
> *9,300-54,900 (Btu/hr)*

Country Stoves, Inc.
1502 14th Street NW
Auburn, WA 98001
(253) 735-1100

> *Non-catalytic models*
> *9,000-70,000 (Btu/hr)*

EarthStove, Inc.
10595 SW Manhasset Street
Tualatin, OR 97062
(503) 692-3991

> *Catalytic models*
> *6,500-74,126 (Btu/hr)*
>
> *Non-catalytic models*
> *11,500-48,100 (Btu/hr)*

England's Stove Works, Inc.
P. O. Box 206
Monroe, VA 24574
(804) 929-0120

> *Catalytic models*
> *7,200-35,600 (Btu/hr)*

Fireplace Products International
6988 Venture Street
Delta, BC V4G-1H4
Canada
(604) 946-5155

> *Non-catalytic models*
> *5,900-59,000 (Btu/hr)*

Harman Stove Co.
352 Mountain House Road
Halifax, PA 17032
(717) 362-9080

> *Non-catalytic model*
> *70,000 (Btu/hr)*

Heat Tech Industries
P. O. Box 727
Biggs, CA 95917
(530) 846-1985

> *Non-catalytic models*
> *11,300-35,800 (Btu/hr)*

———◆———

High Valley Stoves
Route 3, Box 288-A
Bakersville, NC 28705
(828) 765-6850

Catalytic models
2,000-45,000 (Btu/hr)

Non-catalytic model
45,000 (Btu/hr)

Hitzer, Inc.
269 East Main Street
Berne, IN 46711
(219) 589-8536

Non-catalytic models
16,000-95,000 (Btu/hr)

Jotul, Inc.
400 Riverside Street
Portland, ME 04104
(207) 797-5912

Catalytic models
8,880-35,100 (Btu/hr)

JC's Stoves & Ironworks
13736 South Locan Street
Selma, CA 93662
(209) 896-8445

Catalytic models
12,100-65,200 (Btu/hr)

Kirkland Fireplace Dist.
Suite 11
12700 NE 124th Street
Kirkland, WA 98034
(425) 821-4800

Catalytic models
10,700-75,700 (Btu/hr)

Martin Industries, Inc.
301 East Tennessee Street
P. O. Box 128
Florence, AL 35631
(256) 767-0330

Catalytic models
5,200-38,900 (Btu/hr)

NHC, Inc.
Hearthstone Way
Morrisville, VT 05661
(802) 888-5232

Non-catalytic models
40,000-80,000 (Btu/hr)

OK Doke, Ltd.
1425 Weld County Road 32
Longmont, CO 80504
(303) 776-2300

Catalytic models
9,900-20,000 (Btu/hr)

Oregon Woodstoves, Inc.
1844 Main Street
Springfield, OR 97477
(541) 747-8868

Catalytic models
7,800-40,000 (Btu/hr)

Orley's Manufacturing Co.
300 S Craterlick Highway
Medford, OR 97503
(541) 779-5240

Catalytic models
9,100-39,000 (Btu/hr)

Orrville Products, Inc.
375 East Orr Street
P. O. Box 902
Orrville, OH 44667-0902
(800) 232-4010

Catalytic models
11,200-68,900 (Btu/hr)

Non-catalytic models
7,200-48,600 (Btu/hr)

Osburn Manufacturing, Inc.
6670 Butter Crescent
Saanichton, BC V8M-2G8
Canada
(250) 652-4200

Non-catalytic models
9,000-100,000 (Btu/hr)

Pacific Energy Woodstoves, Ltd.
P. O. Box 1060
Duncan, BC V9L-3Y2
Canada
(250) 748-1184

Non-catalytic models
0,600-36,400 (Btu/hr)

Pierce Engineered Products
P. O. Box 10107
Eugene, OR 90414
(541) 485-0063

Non-catalytic models
10,000-61,400 (Btu/hr)

Pyro Industries, Inc.
695 Pease Road
Burlington, WA 98233
(360) 757-9728

> *Non-catalytic models*
> *9,000-35,700 (Btu/hr)*

Reverso Manufacturing, Ltd.
790 Rowntree Dairy Road
Woodbridge, ON L4L-5V3
Canada
(416) 748-3064

> *Non-catalytic models*
> *11,200-33,800 (Btu/hr)*

Russo Products, Inc.
61 Pleasant Street
Randolph, MA 02368
(781) 963-1182

> *Catalytic models*
> *7,900-40,900 (Btu/hr)*

Sherwood Industries, Ltd.
6782 Old Field Road
Saanichton, BC V8M-2A3
Cananda
(250) 652-3223

> *Non-catalytic models*
> *10,200-31,100 (Btu/hr)*

Travis Industries, Inc.
10850 117th Place NE
Kirkland, WA 98033
(425) 827-9505

> *Non-catalytic models*
> *66,000-74,300 (Btu/hr)*

Vermont Castings, Inc.
P. O. Box 501
Bethel, VT 05032
(802) 234-2300

Catalytic models
24,000-54,000 (Btu/hr)

Non-catalytic model
40,000 (Btu/hr)

Welenco Stove Store
533 Thain Road
Lewiston, ID 83501-5532
(208) 743-5525

Non-catalytic models
9,600-23,900 (Btu/hr)

Wolf Steel, Ltd.
9 Napoleon Road
Barrie, ON L4M-4Y8
Canada
(705) 721-1212

Non-catalytic models
10,200-31,100 (Btu/hr)

Woodstock Soapstone Co.
RR1, Box 37H
Air Park Road
West Lebanon, NH 03784
(603) 298-5955

Catalytic models
13,200-40,000 (Btu/hr)

Western Fab and Finish, Inc.
1st & A Streets
Airport Road
Walla Walla, WA 99362
509-529-9820

*Catalytic models
6,800–57,100 (Btu/hr)*

*Non-catalytic model
12,200–33,700 (Btu/hr)*

Winston Stove Company
13643 Fifth Street
Chino, CA 91710
714-591-7405

*Non-catalytic models
9,700–29,400 (Btu/hr)*

Wolf Steel Ltd.
RR1 (Highways 11 & 23)
Barrie, ON L4M 4Y8
Canada
705-721-1212

*Non-catalytic models
10,200–31,100 (Btu/hr)*

Woodkiln Inc.
24 Jamestown Street
Sinclairville, NY 14782
716-962-8178

*Non-catalytic model
10,700–27,200 (Btu/hr)*

Woodstock Soapstone Company, Inc.
RR1, Box 37H
Air Park Road
West Lebanon, NH 03784
603-298-5955

*Catalytic model
13,200–40,000 (Btu/hr)*

Courtesy: *The Environmental
Protection Agency*

INDEX

(Illustrations are indicated by page numbers in *italics;* charts and tables are
indicated by page numbers in **bold.**)